بسم الله الرحمن الرحيم

A REAL SKETCH OF THE PROPHET MUHAMMAD ﷺ

The Perfect Exemplar for Humanity

A Real Sketch of the Prophet Muhammad ﷺ

The Perfect Exemplar for Humanity

Minhaj-ul-Quran International

Published by
Minhaj-ul-Quran Publications
30 Brindley Road
Manchester
M16 9HQ

Editorial Team
Muhammad Farooq Rana, Waqas Ahmed Amin
and Mamoona Umair

ISBN: 978-1-913553-09-8 [Pakistan]
ISBN: 978-1-913553-11-1 [UK]

www.minhaj.org | www.minhajuk.org
www.minhajpublications.com

First published February 2021 [Pakistan]
Second published February 2021 [India]
Third published April 2021 [UK]

Printed by Mega Printing in Turkey

Traits of Islam

LOVE MERCY
COMPASSION
KINDNESS
LIBERALNESS
TOLERANCE
BENEVOLENCE
FORGIVENESS
FORBEARANCE
ALTRUISM
CHARITY
PEACE
MODERATION

The Holy Prophet's

His teachings reflect:

1. Facilitating Ease

REMOVING HARDSHIPS
LIGHTENING BURDENS
CREATING COMFORT
GIVING GUIDANCE
HELPING OTHERS

He strictly condemned extremism in all its forms.

2. Moderation

B A L A N C E
MIDDLE PATH/AVOIDING EXTREMES
RECIPROCATING EVIL WITH GOOD
STRIVING FOR PEACE
AND SHOWING COMPASSION
WORKING FOR RECONCILIATION

He is the Ideal Example for Humanity.

Character is Mercy

3. Tolerance

LOVE
KINDNESS
FORGIVENESS
PATIENCE
RESPECTFULNESS

A model of immense Patience and Gentleness.

4. Leniency

GENTLENESS
GENEROSITY
BENEVOLENCE
CLEMENCY
OVERLOOKING
OTHERS' FLAWS

He is the Most Generous, Hospitable and Welcoming for all.

Contents

Part I

General Description of the Personality of the Most Perfect and Beautiful Human: The Holy Prophet Muhammad ﷺ

The Holy Prophet Muhammad ﷺ was the most perfect human being. He was born in the city of Mecca in Arabia, during the early hours of Monday, the twelfth of Rabīʿ al-Awwal in the year of the Elephant (570 ad)—fifty-two days after the armies of Abraha advanced to destroy the *Kaʿba*.

1. His Creation: God Most High, in His mercy, sent His Beloved ﷺ as a mercy to the universe. Prophet Muhammad ﷺ was the one whose soul God created the first. It was created through the direct blessing of God's light, before anything else of the universe had come into existence. It is reported that the Prophet ﷺ said: "The first creation that God brought into existence was the light of your prophet from His light."[1]
2. Light of the Prophet ﷺ means his enlightened and illuminating soul. Whereas being created from the light of God, does not tell that it was a part of God's light or it emerged from God's light. Glory be to Him. God Almighty Himself is not light. Instead, He is the Creator of light.
3. Creating from His light implies that God Almighty created the Prophet Muhammad's soul as His first creation of the universe without any intermediary means, as usual in the process of creation, for nonc amongst His creation existed at that time.
4. The expression "from His light", refers to glorification of a particular divine act, to mention the highly esteemed and exceptionally honoured status of the blessed one, who has been miraculously created, through the special grace of the Lord Almighty.

[1] Set forth by •ʿAbd al-Razzāq in *al-Muṣannaf (al-Juzʾ al-Mafqūd)*, 1:63 §63. •al-Qasṭallānī in *al-Mawāhib al-Laduniyya bi al-Minḥ al-Muḥammadiyya*, 1:71. •al-Ḥalabī in *al-Sīra al-Ḥalabiyya*, 1:50.

5. A similar style of expression has been used in the Qur'ān, mentioning the creation of Adam, Jesus and human beings. It is stated regarding the creation of humans: ﴾*Then He proportioned him and breathed into him of His spirit.*﴿ [Q.32:9.]

It is stated regarding the creation of Adam: ﴾*So when I have proportioned him and blown into him from My spirit, then fall down in prostration before him (in his honour).*﴿ [Q.38:72.]

The similar expression has been used for the creation of Jesus: ﴾*The Messiah, Jesus, son of Maryam (Mary) was only Allah's Messenger, and His Word, which He conveyed to Maryam (Mary), and a Spirit from Him. So believe in Allah and His messengers and do not say: 'Three'. Refrain (from this belief). It is better for you. Indeed Allah is Only One God.*﴿ [Q.4:171.]

6. Therefore, this miraculous and blessed creation of the light (soul) of the most beloved and esteemed Prophet Muhammad ﷺ has been mentioned in another hadith, in the words: "The first creation that Allah brought into existence was my light (soul)."[1]
7. He was the first of all the Prophets ﷺ, as he said: "I was a Prophet when Adam was between soul and body."[2]
8. He was also the last of all Prophets ﷺ, as he said: "I was the first Prophet in creation, and the last of them in raising."[3]

---

[1] Set forth by •al-Ḥalabī in *Insān al-ʿUyūn fī Sīra al-Amīn al-Maʾmūn*, 1:240.

[2] Set forth by •Ibn Abī Shayba in *al-Muṣannaf*, 7:329 §36553. •Ibn Abī Saʿd in *al-Ṭabaqāt al-Kubrā*, 1:148.

[3] Set forth by •al-Ṭabarānī in *Musnad al-Shāmiyyīn*, 4:34–35 §2662. •Tamām al-Rāzī in *al-Fawāʾid*, 2:15 §1003. •al-Baghawī in *Maʿālim al-Tanzīl*, 3:508.

9. He said: "I am the last of all prophets and no other prophet or messenger would be raised after me.[1] He further explained that the Divine process of raising the prophets and messengers has been completed and stopped with my raising."[2]

10. He said: "I have completed the construction of the palace of the prophethood and there is no space left for any other brick to be placed in it.[3]

11. He grew an orphan as his father, ʿAbd Allāh, died before he was born and his mother, Āmina, died when he was a young child.

12. HIS PHYSICAL APPEARANCE: He had broad shoulders[4] and a broad high chest. He was strongly built; his chest and stomach were flat and firm. No part of his flesh was loose.[5] On his back, between his shoulders, was the Seal of Prophethood.[6] His complexion was white tinged with

---

[1] Set forth by •al-Tirmidhī in *al-Sunan*, 4:499 §2219.

[2] Set forth by •Ibn Ḥibbān in *al-Ṣaḥīḥ*, 14:316 §6406.

[3] Set forth by •al-Bukhārī in *al-Ṣaḥīḥ*, 3:1300 §3341–3342. •Muslim in *al-Ṣaḥīḥ*, 4:1791 §§2286–2287.

[4] Set forth by •al-Bukhārī in *al-Ṣaḥīḥ*, 3:1303 §3358. •Muslim in *al-Ṣaḥīḥ*, 4:1818 §2337. •Aḥmad b. Ḥanbal in *al-Musnad*, 4:281 §18496. •al-Tirmidhī in *al-Shamāʾil al-Muḥammadiyya wa Khaṣāʾiṣ al-Muṣṭafwiyya*, p. 30 §3.

[5] Set forth by •al-Tirmidhī in *al-Shamāʾil al-Muḥammadiyya wa Khaṣāʾiṣ al-Muṣṭafwiyya*, p. 36 §8. •Ibn Ḥibbān in *al-Thiqāt*, 2:145–146. •al-Ṭabarānī in *al-Muʿjam al-Kabīr*, 22:155 §414. •Ibn Saʿd in *al-Ṭabaqāt al-Kubrā*, 1:422. •al-Bayhaqī in *Dalāʾil al-Nubuwwa*, 1:304.

[6] Set forth by •al-Bukhārī in *al-Ṣaḥīḥ*, 3:1301 §3348. •Muslim in *al-Ṣaḥīḥ*, 4:1823 §2345–2346.

reddishness,[1] like a flower. When he took his shirt off his shoulders, the colour of his body was like cast silver.[2]

His neck was like a column of silver.[3] His teeth were perfectly white and even, with a slight space between them.[4]

When he was happy, his face shone like the moon,[5] and when he spoke, it seemed as if a light emanated from between his teeth.[6] He had big but beautiful hands and feet. The palms of his hands and the soles of his feet were firmly padded.[7] He had no hair on his feet. When he washed them, the water didn't stay on them.[8]

He walked with a firm gait, slightly leaning forward as if he were striding downhill.[9] He could walk very fast. People would run behind him and could not keep pace with

---

[1] Set forth by •Aḥmad b. Ḥanbal in *al-Musnad*, 1:116 §944. •al-Rūyānī in *al-Musnad*, 2:318 §1280. Ibn Saʿd in *al-Ṭabaqāt al-Kubrā*, 1:416. •al-Tirmidhī in *al-Shamāʾil al-Muḥammadiyya wa Khaṣāʾiṣ al-Muṣṭafwiyya*, p. 40 §12. •al-Bayhaqī in *Dalāʾil al-Nubuwwa*, 1:241.

[2] Set forth by •al-Tirmidhī in *al-Shamāʾil al-Muḥammadiyya*, p. 40 §12. •al-Bayhaqī in *Dalāʾil al-Nubuwwa*, 1:241.

[3] Set forth by •al-Tirmidhī in *al-Shamāʾil al-Muḥammadiyya wa Khaṣāʾiṣ al-Muṣṭafwiyya*, p. 36 §8. •Ibn Ḥibbān in *al-Thiqāt*, 2:146. •al-Ṭabarānī in *al-Muʿjam al-Kabīr*, 22:155 §414.

[4] Set forth by •al-Dārimī in *al-Sunan*, 1:44 §58. •al-Tirmidhī in *al-Shamāʾil al-Muḥammadiyya wa Khaṣāʾiṣ al-Muṣṭafwiyya*, p. 41 §15. •al-Ṭabarānī in *al-Muʿjam al-Awsaṭ*, 1:235 §767.

[5] Set forth by •al-Bukhārī in *al-Ṣaḥīḥ*, 3:1305 §3363. •Muslim in *al-Ṣaḥīḥ*, 4:2127 §2769.

[6] Set forth by •al-Dārimī in *al-Sunan*, 1:44 §58. •al-Tirmidhī in *al-Shamāʾil al-Muḥammadiyya wa Khaṣāʾiṣ al-Muṣṭafwiyya*, p. 41 §15.

[7] Set forth by •al-Bukhārī in *al-Ṣaḥīḥ*, 5:2212 §5567.

[8] Set forth by •al-Tirmidhī in *al-Shamāʾil al-Muḥammadiyya wa Khaṣāʾiṣ al-Muṣṭafwiyya*, p. 37 §8. •Ibn Ḥibbān in *al-Thiqāt*, 2:146. •al-Ṭabarānī in *al-Muʿjam al-Kabīr*, 22:155–156 §414.

[9] Set forth by •Aḥmad b. Ḥanbal in *al-Musnad*, 1:127 §1053. •al-Tirmidhī in *al-Sunan*, 5:598 §3637.

him.[1] When people who were weak were travelling with him, he slowed down for them, or made them ride animals, and he prayed for them.

He insisted that his Companions ﷺ should walk in front of him rather than behind him.[2] His face was the most beautiful of human faces. His form was the most beautiful to be found among men;[3] so was his character.

General Description of Prophet Muhammad's ﷺ Beautiful Being and Lovely Manners

13. He was the most generous, the most kind, the most gentle, the most valorous and the most humble. He cast his eyes down more often than up and appeared shyer than a well-sheltered young girl.[4]
14. He would stay silent for long periods and laugh little, yet he had a sense of humour and liked to see others smile.[5]
15. When he was with other people, he would not leave their company until they left, and when he took someone's hand, he would not withdraw his hand until the other person released it. When someone whispered into his ear something that he did not want others to hear, he would not pull his face away until the other did.[6]

---

[1] Set forth by •Aḥmad b. Ḥanbal in *al-Musnad*, 2:350, 380 §§8588, 8930. •al-Tirmidhī in *al-Sunan*, 5:604 §3648.

[2] Set forth by •Aḥmad b. Ḥanbal in *al-Musnad*, 3:397–398 §15316. •al-Dārimī in *al-Sunan*, 1:35–37, §45.

[3] Set forth by •al-Bukhārī in *al-Ṣaḥīḥ*, 3:1303 §3356. •Muslim in *al-Ṣaḥīḥ*, 4:1819, §2337.

[4] Set forth by •al-Bukhārī in *al-Ṣaḥīḥ*, 5:2263 §5751. •Muslim in *al-Ṣaḥīḥ*, 4:1809, §2320.

[5] Set forth by •Aḥmad b. Ḥanbal in *al-Musnad*, 5:86 §20829. •al-Ṭayālisī in *al-Musnad*, 1:105 §771.

[6] Set forth by •Ibn Saʿd in *al-Ṭabaqāt al-Kubrā*, 1:378. •Abū al-Shaykh al-Aṣbahānī in *Akhlāq al-Nabī ﷺ wa Ādābihi*, 1:211 §59. •Abū Nuʿaym in *Ḥilya al-Awliyāʾ*, 3:26.

16. He was very compassionate and loving, especially to women, weak and children. When he promised something to someone, he would fulfil his promise without fail at the first opportunity.[1]
17. He was blessed with such divine grace, beauty and glory, when he sat with his people, they sat around him in a circle, and in love and fascination they would be so quiet and still that if a bird had sat on their heads, it would not have flown away.[2]
18. When something that greatly pleased him was announced to him, he would immediately prostrate as a gesture of thankfulness to God, and his face would shine like the full moon.[3] When he began speaking, he would always smile.[4]
19. In all his relationships he never caused two people to be angry at each other.[5]
20. Whenever he was asked for something, he would give it if he had it. If he did not have it, he would not refuse, but would try to manage it for the needy.[6] He never said no.[7]

---

[1] Set forth by •al-Bukhārī in *al-Ṣaḥīḥ*, 5:1987 §4890. •Aḥmad b. Ḥanbal in *al-Musnad*, 2:185 §6733. •Ibn Mājah in *al-Sunan*, 2:1329 §4010. •Ibn Ḥibbān in *al-Ṣaḥīḥ*, 11:444 §5058. •Abū Dāwūd in *al-Sunan*, 3:82 §2758.

[2] Set forth by •Aḥmad b. Ḥanbal in *al-Musnad*, 4:278 §18476–18477. •Abū Dāwūd in *al-Sunan*, 4:3 §3855. •al-Ṭabarānī in *al-Muʿjam al-Awsaṭ*, 8:5 §7782.

[3] Set forth by •al-Bukhārī in *al-Ṣaḥīḥ*, 3:1305 §3363. •Muslim in *al-Ṣaḥīḥ*, 4:2127 §2769. •Aḥmad b. Ḥanbal in *al-Musnad*, 3:458 §15827.

[4] Set forth by •Abū al-Shaykh al-Aṣbahānī in *Akhlāq al-Nabī ﷺ wa Ādābihi*, 2:17 §207.

[5] Set forth by •al-Bukhārī in *al-Ṣaḥīḥ*, 5:2253 §5718. •Muslim in *al-Ṣaḥīḥ*, 4:1983 §2559.

[6] Set forth by •al-Tirmidhī in *al-Shamāʾil Muḥammadiyya*, p. 294 §356. •al-Maqdisī in *al-Aḥādīth al-Mukhtāra*, 1:181 §88. •Ibn Abī al-Dunyā in *Makārim al-Akhlāq*, p. 118 §390.

[7] Set forth by •al-Bukhārī in *al-Ṣaḥīḥ*, 5:2244 §5687. •Muslim in *al-Ṣaḥīḥ*, 4:1805 §2311.

21. When he was asked to do something, if it was possible, he would say yes. If it was not possible, he would keep silent.[1]

22. He did not approach nor listen to people from whom he expected to hear bad talk, and he did not accept people's talking against each other.[2]

23. He spoke very clearly, separating each word, so that one could easily count word if one cared to.[3]

24. He did not like people to be loud and rude. He loved people who spoke softly.[4]

25. When he knew of something bad anyone had done, he would not while advising mention his name, saying "Why so-and-so has done this?" Instead, he would say, "Why do people do this?"[5]

26. What he hated most was lying. He felt upset if someone spoke the slightest untruth.[6]

---

[1] Set forth by •al-Tirmidhī in *al-Shamā'il Muḥammadiyya*, p. 278 §337. •al-Ṭabarānī in *al-Mu'jam al-Kabīr*, 22:158 §414.

[2] Set forth by •al-Tirmidhī in *al-Shamā'il Muḥammadiyya*, p. 278 §337.•al-Ṭabarānī in *al-Mu'jam al-Kabīr*, 22:158 §414; & in *al-Aḥādīth al-Ṭawāl*, 1:245 §29. •Ibn 'Asākir in *Tārīkh Madīna Dimashq*, 3:350. •al-Bayhaqī in *Shu'ab al-Īmān*, 2:156 §1430; & in *Dalā'il al-Nubuwwa*, 1:290. •al-Haythamī in *Majma' al-Zawā'id*, 8:274.

[3] Set forth by •al-Bukhārī in *al-Ṣaḥīḥ*, 3:1307 §3374. •Muslim in *al-Ṣaḥīḥ*, 4:2298 §2493.

[4] Set forth by •al-Bukhārī in *al-Ṣaḥīḥ*, 5:2242 §5678. •Muslim in *al-Ṣaḥīḥ*, 4:2003 §2592.

[5] Set forth by •Abū Dāwūd in *al-Sunan*, 4:250 §4788. •al-Nasā'ī in *al-Sunan*, 6:60 §3217. •al-Ḥākim in *al-Mustadrak*, 4:84 §6958. •al-Bayhaqī in *Shu'ab al-Īmān*, 6:265 §8099.

[6] Set forth by •al-Tirmidhī in *al-Sunan*, 4:348 §1973. •Isḥāq b. Rāhawayh in *al-Musnad*, 3:654 §1245. •al-Bayhaqī in *Shu'ab al-Īmān*, 4:208 §4815.

27. He was loving and gentle in his words and his being,[1] even to the worst of the people and so gained their hearts.[2]
28. When he did not see one of his people for three days, he would ask after that person, and if absent people could not come, he would go to them.[3]
29. When he would take someone's hand to say farewell, he would not withdraw his hand before the other withdrew his, and he would pray, "I entrust you to God's care, you and your faith and your trust and your deeds and your end."[4]
30. He was very careful of the cloth that was used in his robes. If it contained silk, he would discard it.[5] He liked wool. He had a woollen robe that he wore on Fridays and holy days.[6]
31. When groups of foreigners came to visit him, he would wear his best clothes in their honour, and ask his companions to do the same.[7]
32. He liked to use the *miswāk*, a stick of wood beaten into fibres at one end, as a toothbrush. He carried it with him and used it to clean his teeth very often. He would not go to bed, without brushing his teeth.[8]

---

[1] Set forth by •al-Bukhārī in *al-Ṣaḥīḥ*, 1:226 §602. •Muslim in *al-Ṣaḥīḥ*, 3:1692 §2150.

[2] Set forth by •al-Bukhārī in *al-Ṣaḥīḥ*, 3:1148 §2980. •Muslim in *al-Ṣaḥīḥ*, 2:730 §1057.

[3] Set forth by •Abū Yaʿlā in *al-Musnad*, 6:150 §3429. •al-Aṣbahānī in *Akhlāq al-Nabī wa Ādābihi*, 1:446 §165.

[4] Set forth by •al-Tirmidhī in *al-Sunan*, 5:499 §3442.

[5] Set forth by •al-Bukhārī in *al-Ṣaḥīḥ*, 1:147 §368. •Aḥmad b. Ḥanbal in *al-Musnad*, 1:96 §750. •Abū Dāwūd in *al-Sunan*, 4:50 §4057.

[6] Set forth by •al-Bayhaqī in *Maʿrifa al-Sunan wa al-Āthār*, 3:32 §1875. •Abū Ḥayyān al-Aṣbahānī in *Akhlāq al-Nabī* ﷺ *wa Ādābihi*, 2:172 §292.

[7] Set forth by •Ibn Saʿd in *al-Ṭabaqāt al-Kubrā*, 4:346. •Abū Ḥayyān al-Aṣbahānī in *Akhlāq al-Nabī* ﷺ *wa Ādābihi*, 2:151 §280.

[8] Set forth by •al-Bukhārī in *al-Ṣaḥīḥ*, 1:382 §1085. •Muslim in *al-Ṣaḥīḥ*, 1:220 §§§§252–255. •Aḥmad b. Ḥanbal in *al-Musnad*, 6:188

33. When he drank, he would breathe before swallowing, and say: 'In the name of God the Beneficent, the Compassionate.' After each swallow he would say: 'Praise is due to God.' He would take only two or three swallows in this way.[1]

34. He liked to drink water from its source. Sometimes he would send people to particular springs, wells and fountains, and he would pray for the people who brought the water to him.[2]

35. He liked to sit and watch running water and greenery.[3]

36. He ate little,[4] and if he ate in the evening he would not eat in the morning.[5] He ate only when he was hungry and stopped eating before he was full.[6]

37. He fasted often. In addition to the month of *Ramaḍān*, the month in which he fasted the most was Shaʿbān.[7]

38. Sometimes he would fast for days without breaking the fast, but he would forbid others to do that.[8]

---

§25594. •Abū Dāwūd in *al-Sunan*, 1:15 §57.

[1] Set forth by •al-Bukhārī in *al-Ṣaḥīḥ*, 5:2133 §5308. •Muslim in *al-Ṣaḥīḥ*, 3:1603 §2028. •al-Tirmidhī in *al-Sunan*, 4:302 §1884–1885. •al-Ṭabarānī in *al-Muʿjam al-Kabīr*, 10:205 §10475.

[2] Set forth by •Ibn Saʿd in *al-Ṭabaqāt al-Kubrā*, 1:504. •al-Suyūṭī in *al-Shamāʾil al-Sharīfa*, p. 312 §574. •al-Munāwī in *Fayḍ al-Qadīr*, 5:218.

[3] Set forth by •al-Tirmidhī in *al-Sunan*, 2:155 §334. •Ibn Tamām al-Rāzī in *al-Fawāʾid*, 2:107 §1268. •al-Suyūṭī in *al-Shamāʾil al-Sharīfa*, p. 311 §573.

[4] Set forth by •al-Bukhārī in *al-Ṣaḥīḥ*, 5:2061 §5078.

[5] Set forth by •al-Ṭabarānī in *Musnad al-Shāmiyyīn*, 1:374 §650. •Abū Nuʿaym in *Ḥilya al-Awliyāʾ*, 3:323. •al-Bayhaqī in *Shuʿab al-Īmān*, 5:26 §5644.

[6] Set forth by •Aḥmad b. Ḥanbal *al-Musnad*, 4:132 §17225. •al-Tirmidhī in *al-Sunan*, 4:590 §2380.

[7] Set forth by •Aḥmad b. Ḥanbal in *al-Musnad*, 6:84 §24586. •al-Tirmidhī in *al-Sunan*, 3:113 §736.

[8] Set forth by •al-Bukhārī in *al-Ṣaḥīḥ*, 2:678 §1822. •Muslim in *al-Ṣaḥīḥ*, 2:774 §1102.

39. He never kept anything for tomorrow. Sometimes neither he nor his family had anything to eat for days. They often ate barley bread.[1]

40. When he broke his fast at sunset, he would first eat a date or two or drink water before he made his sunset prayer.[2]

41. When he ate, he sat on the floor;[3] he never leaned on anything while he ate.[4] He washed his hands well before and after eating.[5]

42. He ate what was on his side of the plate; he never reached for a morsel in the middle of the plate.[6]

43. He did not start eating a warm dish until it cooled a bit. He said, "Eat cold food, because it has the blessing of abundance. If you are heedful you will see how much more you must eat when you eat warm food..."[7]

44. He never blew on his food to cool it, nor did he blow into his cup when he drank.[8]

45. He preferred the meat of the front part of the sheep.[9] He disliked eating the internal organs of the animal. He refused

---

[1] Set forth by •al-Tirmidhī in *al-Sunan*, 4:580 §2359–2362. •Ibn Ḥibbān in *al-Ṣaḥīḥ*, 14:270 §6356.

[2] Set forth by •Aḥmad b. Ḥanbal in *al-Musnad*, 3:164 §12698. •Abū Dāwūd in *al-Sunan*, 2:306 §2356. •al-Tirmidhī in *al-Sunan*, 3:79 §696.

[3] Set forth by •al-Ṭabarānī in *Muʿjam al-Kabīr*, 12:67 §12494. •al-Bayhaqī in *Shuʿab al-Īmān*, 6:290 §8192.

[4] Set forth by •al-Bukhārī in *al-Ṣaḥīḥ*, 5:2062 §5083.

[5] Set forth by •Ibn Mājah in *al-Sunan*, 2:1085 §3260.

[6] Set forth by •al-Bukhārī in *al-Ṣaḥīḥ*, 5:2056 §§§5061–5063. •Muslim in *al-Ṣaḥīḥ*, 3:1599 §2022. •Abū Ḥayyān al-Aṣbahānī in *Akhlāq al-Nabī ﷺ wa Ādābihi*, 3:201, 210 §§589, 595.

[7] Set forth by •al-Ḥākim in *al-Mustadrak*, 4:132 §7125. •al-Ṭabarānī in *al-Muʿjam al-Kabīr*, 24:66 §172.

[8] Set forth by •al-Bukhārī in *al-Ṣaḥīḥ*, 5:2133 §5307. •Muslim in *Ṣaḥīḥ*, 1:225 §267. •Abū Dāwūd in *al-Sunan*, 3:338 §3728. •al-Tirmidhī in *al-Sunan*, 4:304 §1888.

[9] Set forth by •Aḥmad b. Ḥanbal in *al-Musnad*, 6:8 §23910.

to eat the kidneys, although he did not forbid others to eat them.[1]

Among vegetables he liked squash and cucumbers.[2]

46. He accepted all invitations to dinner, even from a slave, where he may have eaten stale animal fat with old barley bread.[3] He started eating only after others started. After each meal he said: "Praise is due to God" and prayed for his host and the ones who had shared the meal.[4]

47. He went to bed after the night prayer, awoke in the middle of the night to pray, and slept again until before the morning prayer.[5] His eyes slept but his heart did not sleep.[6]

48. His bed was piece of felt.[7] Sometimes he used a straw mat thrown on the hard floor, which marked his blessed side when he lay upon it.[8] The mat was not bigger than the size of a grave.[9]

He would not go to bed without taking an ablution and cleaning his teeth.[10]

---

[1] Set forth by •Abū al-Faḍl al-ʿIrāqī in *al-Mughnī ʿan Ḥaml al-Asfār*, 1:655 §2439. •al-Kāsānī in *Badāʾiʿ al-Ṣanāʾiʿ*, 5:61. •al-Ghazālī in *Iḥyāʾ ʿUlūm al-Dīn*, 2:372.

[2] Set forth by •Muslim in *al-Ṣaḥīḥ*, 3:1615 §2041. •al-Tirmidhī in *al-Sunan*, 4:284 §1850; & in *Shamāʾil al-Muḥammadiyya*, p. 168 §203. •al-Ṭabarānī in *al-Muʿjam al-Kabīr*, 24:274 §697.

[3] Set forth by •Muslim in *al-Ṣaḥīḥ*, 4:2198 §2865. •al-Tirmidhī in *al-Sunan*, 3:337 §1017.

[4] Set forth by •Muslim in *al-Ṣaḥīḥ*, 3:1615 §2042.

[5] Set forth by •al-Bukhārī in *al-Ṣaḥīḥ*, 1:385 §§1095–1096. •Muslim in *al-Ṣaḥīḥ*, 1:509–510 §§738–739.

[6] Set forth by •al-Bukhārī in *al-Ṣaḥīḥ*, 1:385 §1096. •Muslim in *al-Ṣaḥīḥ*, 1:509 §738.

[7] Set forth by •al-Bukhārī in *al-Ṣaḥīḥ*, 5:2371 §6091. •Muslim in *al-Ṣaḥīḥ*, 3:1650 §2082.

[8] Set forth by •Aḥmad b. Ḥanab in *al-Musnad*, 3:139–140 §12440. •Abū Yaʿlā in *al-Musnad*, 5:167 §2782.

[9] Set forth by •Abū Dāwūd in *al-Sunan*, 4:310 §5044.

[10] Set forth by •al-Bukhārī in *al-Ṣaḥīḥ*, 1:97 §244. •Muslim in *al-Ṣaḥīḥ*,

49. He slept with his head turned in the direction of the *Kaʿba.*[1] He slept on his right side and used his right hand as a pillow, placing his palm under his cheek. Before he fell asleep, he would pray: "O my Sustainer, I live with Your name; I die with Your name."[2]

Then he would repeat three times: 'On the day of Resurrection, save me from Your wrath.'[3]

50. He liked to give gifts and advised his people to do the same. He would say that giving gifts bring people together.[4]

51. He smiled when he spoke and showed care and compassion to the members of his household.[5] He did not touch even the hand of a woman from outside his family.[6]

52. He would talk to, amuse and play with his wives. He would show them affection, love and concern.[7]

53. He helped with the household chores. He cleaned, washed, mended and milked the sheep. No work was beneath his dignity.[8]

4:2081 §2710. •al-Ṭabarānī in *al-Muʿjam al-Awsaṭ*, 8:67 §7980. •Abū Nuʿaym in *Maʿrifat al-Ṣaḥāba*, 5:2592 §6247.

[1] Set forth by •Muslim in *al-Ṣaḥīḥ*, 1:476 §683. •Aḥmad b. Ḥanbal in *al-Musnad*, 5:309 §22685.

[2] Set forth by •al-Bukhārī in *al-Ṣaḥīḥ*, 5:2327 §5955. •Muslim in *al-Ṣaḥīḥ*, 4:2083 §2711.

[3] Set forth by•Aḥmad b. Ḥanbal in *al-Musnad*, 6:288 §26508. •Abū Dāwūd in *al-Sunan*, 4:310 §5045. •al-Tirmidhī in *al-Sunan*, 5:471 §3399.

[4] Set forth by •Aḥmad b. Ḥanbal in *al-Musnad*, 2:405 §9239. •Abū Dāwūd in *al-Sunan*, 2:128 §1672. •Abū Yaʿlā in *al-Musnad*, 11:9 §6148.

[5] Set forth by •al-Tirmidhī in *al-Sunan*, 5:601 §3641. •Aḥmad b. Ḥanbal in *al-Musnad*, 5:91 §20885. •Isḥāq b. Rāhawayh in *al-Musnad*, 3:1008 §1750.

[6] Set forth by •al-Bukhārī in *al-Ṣaḥīḥ*, 2:967 §2564.

[7] Set forth by •al-Bukhārī in *al-Ṣaḥīḥ*, 5:2004 §4930. •Aḥmad b. Ḥanbal in *al-Musnad*, 3:172 §12784. •Abū Dāwūd in *al-Sunan*, 3:29 §2578.

[8] Set forth by •al-Bukhārī in *al-Ṣaḥīḥ*, 5:229 §5850. •Ibn Ḥibbān in *al-Ṣaḥīḥ*, 14:351 §6440. •al-Ṭabarānī in *al-Muʿjam al-Kabīr*, 12:67 §12494.

54. He took his wives out and brought them and his children to special holy day prayers. When he travelled, he would always allow his family to accompany him.[1]

55. When his wives became ill, he took care of them and cooked soup for them saying, "Drink! This will cleanse the pain and sadness in the heart of the sick as water cleanses the dirt of a person's body."[2]

56. When his wives wanted something, he never said no, but brought them what they wanted as soon as he could.[3]

57. When they were upset, he would be very kind and gentle with them. And asked them to pray so that their grief would subside.[4]

58. He was gentle with his children.[5] He would stand up, as a gesture of respect, when his daughter Fāṭima ﷺ came to see him, and he would kiss the top of her head.[6]

59. His grandchildren would climb on his back while he prayed, and he did not mind.[7] He loved all of his people, but he loved the very young and the very old most of all.[8]

---

[1] Set forth by •al-Bukhārī in *al-Ṣaḥīḥ*, 1:181 §2453. •Muslim in *al-Ṣaḥīḥ*, 3:1609 §2037.

[2] Set forth by •Aḥmad b. Ḥanbal in *al-Musnad*, 6:32 §24081. •al-Tirmidhī in *al-Sunan*, 4:383 §2039. •al-Nasāʾī in *al-Sunan al-Kubrā*, 4:372 §§7573, 7576.

[3] Set forth by •al-Bukhārī in *al-Ṣaḥīḥ*, 5:2048 §5042. •al-Tirmidhī in *al-Sunan*, 3:519 §§1214–1215.

[4] Set forth by •Muslim in *al-Ṣaḥīḥ*, 2:632 §918(4). •Ibn Ḥibbān in *al-Ṣaḥīḥ*, 3:145 §864. •al-Ṭabarānī in *Kitāb al-Duʿāʾ*, p. 313 §1026.

[5] Set forth by •al-Bukhārī in *al-Ṣaḥīḥ*, 1:439 §1241. •Muslim in *al-Ṣaḥīḥ*, 4:1808 §2316.

[6] Set forth by •Abū Dāwūd in *al-Sunan*, 4:355 §5217.

[7] Set forth by •al-Bukhārī in *al-Ṣaḥīḥ*, 1:193 §494. •Aḥmad b. Ḥanbal in *al-Musnad*, 3:493 §16076.

[8] Set forth by •Abū Yaʿlā in *al-Musnad*, 7:205–206 §4195.

60. When he led the prayer, he made it short to make it easy for others. When he prayed alone, he made it long.[1]

61. He would say to the preachers and leaders: 'Speak not long. Long talk has the effect of a sorcerer's spell. Make your preaching short and make things easy for people, not difficult. Give them good tidings, not threats to push them away.'[2]

62. At the time of the morning prayer, the poor and maids of the people of Medina would come to the mosque with water pitchers: he would always bless them.[3]

63. He would say to his Companions ﷺ: 'If anyone is sick, let me go and visit him. If anyone has passed, let me assist at his funeral. If anyone has dreamed, let him come and tell me his dream.'[4]

64. His staunchest enemies became his closest followers when the veil of blind prejudice was removed from their sight, and when they were able, for the very first time, to see with clarity the true nature of the Prophet's character. Thumāma b. Uthāl ﷺ, having been forgiven by the Prophet ﷺ, expressed a sentiment that was shared by many other former enemies of Islam. He said to the Holy Prophet ﷺ: "By God! Throughout the entire earth, no face was more despised by me than your face; and yet now your face has become the most beloved of faces to me. By God! Throughout the entire earth, no religion was more despised by me than your religion; and yet now your religion has become the most beloved of religions to me. By God! Throughout the entire earth, no land was more despised by

[1] Set forth by •al-Bukhārī in *al-Ṣaḥīḥ*, 1:248 §671. •Muslim in *al-Ṣaḥīḥ*, 1:343 §470.

[2] Set forth by •al-Bukhārī in *al-Ṣaḥīḥ*, 1:38 §69. •Abū Dāwūd in *al-Sunan*, 1:289 §§1106–1107.

[3] Set forth by •Muslim in *al-Ṣaḥīḥ*, 4:1812 §2324.

[4] Set forth by •al-Bukhārī in *al-Ṣaḥīḥ*, 1:175–176 §446, 448, 1:471 §1182. •Aḥmad b. Ḥanbal in *al-Musnad*, 5:14 §20177.

me than your land; and yet now your land has become the most beloved of lands to me."[1]

65. In later period, during the Prophet's lifetime, the last holdouts from the Quraysh were deeply moved by the Prophet's forgiveness and generosity. These were people who had shown enmity towards the Prophet ﷺ for many years. In spite of their past evils, and in spite of the fact that the Muslims did not need their help—for Islam by that time had many adherents—the Prophet ﷺ not only forgave them but acted generously towards them as well. For example, the Prophet ﷺ gave one-hundred sheep to Ṣafwān b. *Umma*yya, one of the bitterest foes of Islam. Then during the same meeting, the Prophet ﷺ gave him one-hundred more sheep; and then he gave him yet another one-hundred sheep. At that time, Ṣafwān was a polytheist, but he was so moved by the Prophet's generosity that he embraced Islam. He later said: "May my father and mother be sacrificed for him; by God! I have never seen a better teacher or better teachings before or since; he did not rebuke me, hit me or revile me."

He further stated: "By God! God's Messenger gave me a great deal, and that at a time when he was the most despised of people to me. He then continued to give me more and more until he became the most beloved of people to me."[2]

66. Yet on another occasion, almost an entire tribe embraced Islam as a result of the Prophet's generosity and forgiveness. That story began when a man went to the Prophet ﷺ, intending to assassinate him. God not only protected the Prophet ﷺ from the man's plot, but also, in the end, gave the Prophet ﷺ upper hand over him, so that he could have killed him had he wished. But instead, the Prophet ﷺ forgave him, an act of mercy that had such a profound

[1] Set forth by •al-Bukhārī in *al-Ṣaḥīḥ*, 4:1589 §4114.

[2] Set forth by •Muslim in *al-Ṣaḥīḥ*, 4:1806 §2313.

impact on the man's heart that he embraced Islam. What is more, he went back to his people and conveyed to them the Prophet's message; only a short while passed before a great many of his fellow tribesmen accepted his invitation and became Muslims.[1]

67. The Prophet's message was universal; the truth he conveyed and the character he displayed appealed not only to polytheistic Arab, but to Jews and Christians as well. When the Prophet ﷺ first arrived in Medina, he was visited by the famous Jewish scholar, ʿAbd Allāh b. Salām. ʿAbd Allāh later recounted his first encounter with the Prophet ﷺ: "I went to where the people of Medina were gathered, so that I could see the Messenger of God. When I saw his face, I immediately knew that his was not the face of a liar. And the first thing I heard him say was: "O people, spread greetings of peace, feed others from your food, join ties of family relations, pray at night when people are sleeping, and, as a result of doing all of that, you will enter Paradise in peace."

According to another narration, the Messenger of Allah ﷺ said: "Worship the Sustainer, *al-Raḥmān*, feed others, establish the custom of invoking peace, then you will enter Paradise with security."[2]

68. Another Jewish man, Zayd b. Saʿna, wanted to test the Prophet's patience by doing something harmful to him. The Prophet ﷺ not only forgave Zayd, but also ordered ʿUmar to give Zayd a gift on his behalf. Zayd, who was an eminent Jewish scholar, said: "Just by looking at God's Messenger, I could discern in his face all of the signs of Prophethood, except for two, which could not be discerned simply through the act of looking. Those two signs were,

[1] Set forth by •Aḥmad b. Ḥanbal in *al-Musnad*, 3:364 §14971. •Ibn Ḥibbān in *al-Ṣaḥīḥ*, 7:138 §2883.

[2] Set forth by •Aḥmad b. Ḥanbal in *al-Musnad*, 5:451 §23835. •al-Tirmidhī in *al-Sunan*, 4:652 §2485.

first, his mercy precedes when faced with ignorance, and when the one who wronged him anxiously waits to see whether he shows forbearance or anger, and second, the more ignorance he is confronted with, the more forbearing he becomes. I tested the Prophet ﷺ in order to see whether he possessed these qualities." Answering his own question, Zayd said to ʿUmar (to whom he was recounting the above narrative, "O ʿUmar, I am indeed pleased with God as my Lord, with Islam as my religion, and with Muhammad as my Prophet. And I make your bear witness that I am giving away half of my wealth as charity to the nation of Muhammad."[1]

69. HIS MERCY TOWARDS ALL HUMAN BEINGS: Jarīr b. ʿAbd Allāh ؓ reported that the Messenger of God ﷺ said: "If one is not merciful towards people, then God—the Possessor of Might and Majesty—will not be merciful towards him."[2]

Abū Hurayra ؓ said, "I heard Abū al-Qāsim ﷺ say: "The quality of being merciful (towards others) is not removed except from one who is (truly) miserable."[3]

To be merciful is to have a soft heart; having a soft heart is a sign of faith (*īmān*). Therefore, if one does not have a soft heart, one does not have faith. And if one does not have faith, one is truly miserable.

ʿAbd Allāh b. ʿAmr ؓ related that the Messenger of Allah ﷺ said: "As for the merciful ones, the Most-Merciful One (God) will have mercy on them. Be merciful towards those who are on earth, and the One in (i.e. above) the heavens will be merciful towards you." (The word) *al-raḥim* (relatives by way of the womb) is derived from (the word) al-Raḥmān (the Ever-Merciful). So, if one joins ties with relatives (by way of the womb), God will join ties

[1] Set forth by •al-Ṭabarānī in *al-Muʿjam al-Kabīr* in 5:222–223 §5147.

[2] Set forth by •Aḥmad b. Ḥanbal in *al-Musnad*, 4:358 §19187.

[3] Set forth by •al-Tirmidhī in *al-Sunan*, 4:323 §1923. •Abū Dāwūd in *al-Sunan*, 4:286 §4942.

with him. And if one cuts off those ties, God will cut off ties from him.[1]

70. His Mercy Towards the Old and Children: Anas b. Mālik ؓ said, "An old man once came, wanting to meet the Prophet ﷺ. The people (in the Prophet's gathering) were slow to give the old man space; as a result, the Prophet ﷺ said: "Whoever is not merciful towards the young amongst us and respectful towards the elderly amongst us, is not from us."[2]

71. His Mercy Towards Daughters and Young Girls in General: Abū Saʿīd al-Khuḍrī ؓ reported that the Messenger of God ﷺ said: "Whenever a person has three daughters, three sisters, two daughters, or two sisters; fears God regarding them (their upkeep and in terms of treating them with honour and kindness); and does good to them (by being kind and generous towards them), then that person enters Paradise."[3]

72. His Mercy Towards Orphans: Abū Hurayra ؓ related that the Messenger of God ﷺ said: "If one provides for, takes care of, and raises an orphan—regardless of whether that orphan is a relative of his or not—then I and he will be like these two in Paradise."

Explaining what the Prophet ﷺ meant by "these two," Mālik, one of the narrators of the hadith, pointed to his index and middle fingers.[4]

73. His Mercy Towards Widows and the Poor: Abū Hurayra ؓ reported that the Prophet ﷺ said: "A person who strives to take care of the needs of the widow and the poor man is like one who struggles in the way of God, or like one

---

1 Set forth by •al-Ḥumaydī in *al-Musnad*, 2:269–270 §§591–592.

2 Set forth by •al-Tirmidhī in *al-Sunan*, 4:321 §1919.

3 Set forth by •Aḥmad b. Ḥanbal in *al-Musnad*, 3:42 §11402. •al-Tirmidhī in *al-Sunan*, 4:318 §1912.

4 Set forth by •Muslim in *al-Ṣaḥīḥ*, 4:2287 §2983. •Aḥmad b. Ḥanbal in *al-Musnad*, 2:375 §8868.

who stands during the night (to pray) and fasts during the day."[1]

74. His Mercy Towards Prisoners: Abū Mūsā ﷺ reported that the Messenger of God ﷺ said: "Set prisoners free, feed the hungry and visit the sick."[2]

75. His Mercy Towards the Sick: Thawbān ﷺ reported that the Messenger of God ﷺ said: "Whoever visits a sick person remains among the *khurfa* of Paradise until he returns [from his visit]."

Someone asked, "O Messenger of God, what is the *khurfa* of Paradise?" He ﷺ replied, "[The *khurfa* of Paradise] is its fruits.[3] "Fruits" here is a metaphor for the rewards one earns for visiting his sick Muslim brother.

ʿAlī ﷺ reported that he heard the Messenger of God ﷺ say: "Whenever any Muslim visits a sick Muslim at the beginning of the day, then seventy-thousand angels will continue to send prayers upon him until the evening. And if he visits him in the early evening, then seventy-thousand angels will continue to send prayers upon him until the morning, and he will have a garden in Paradise."[4]

76. His Mercy towards Animals: Abū Hurayra ﷺ related from the Prophet ﷺ the story of a man who found a dog that was so thirsty that it was eating wet soil. The man gave something to drink to the dog, and as a result of his generous and merciful action, God ﷻ forgave him (his sins). Abū Hurayra ﷺ further related that after the Prophet ﷺ told this story, his Companions ﷺ asked, "O Messenger

---

[1] Set forth by •al-Bukhārī in *al-Ṣaḥīḥ*, 5:2047 §5038. •al-Tirmidhī in *al-Sunan*, 4:346 §1969.

[2] Set forth by •Abū Dāwūd in *al-Sunan*, 3:187 §3105. •al-Nasāʾī in *al-Sunan*, 5:202 §8666.

[3] Set forth by •Muslim in *al-Ṣaḥīḥ*, 4:1989 §2568. •Aḥmad b. Ḥanbal in *al-Musnad*, 5:277 §22443.

[4] Set forth by •Aḥmad b. Ḥanbal in *al-Musnad*, 1:118 §955. •al-Tirmidhī in *al-Sunan*, 3:300 §969.

of God, are there rewards for us even in animals (i.e. even in helping animals)?" The Prophet ﷺ said: "There is a reward for each wet liver." That is, a Muslim will receive reward for helping anything that has a wet liver—or in other words, anything that is alive and that has a spirit.[1]

According to Imam Ibn Ḥibbān's wording of this hadith, the Prophet ﷺ said: "God forgave him and admitted him into Paradise."[2]

Abū Hurayra ؓ reported that the Prophet ﷺ said: "An adulteress was forgiven (for her sins). This occurred because, one day, she passed by a dog that was seated at the head of a well, a dog whose thirst almost resulted in its death. The adulteress removed her shoe, tied it to her veil, and then lowered the shoe in to the well in order to draw out some water for the dog."[3]

ʿAbd Allāh b. ʿUmar ؓ related that the Messenger of God ﷺ said: "A woman was punished because of a cat that she kept confined until it died of hunger. As a result of what she did, she entered the Hellfire. That is because she neither fed the cat nor gave it something to drink when she confined it; nor did she leave it [to roam free] so that it could eat from the vermin of the earth."[4]

Shaddād b. Aws ؓ related that the Messenger of God ﷺ said: "Verily, God has written excellence (doing something in an excellent manner). So, if you slaughter (an animal), then slaughter (it) in an excellent manner: Sharpen your

---

[1] Set forth by •al-Bukhārī in *al-Ṣaḥīḥ*, 2:833 §2234, 2:870 §2334. •Muslim in *al-Ṣaḥīḥ*, 4:1761 §2244.

[2] Set forth by •Ibn Ḥibbān in *al-Ṣaḥīḥ*, 2:301 §543.

[3] Set forth by •al-Bukhārī in *al-Ṣaḥīḥ*, 3:1279 §3280. •Muslim in *al-Ṣaḥīḥ*, 4:1761 §2245. •Aḥmad b. Ḥanbal in *al-Musnad*, 2:510 §10629.

[4] Set forth by •al-Bukhārī in *al-Ṣaḥīḥ*, 2:834 §2236. •Muslim in *al-Ṣaḥīḥ*, 4:1760 §2242. •al-Dārimī in *al-Sunan*, 2:426 §2814.

blade and thus make matters easy and more comfortable for the animal you are slaughtering."[1]

ʿAbd Allāh b. ʿAmr 🙏 reported that the Messenger of God 🙏 said: "If anyone kills a sparrow or anything above it (in size or significance), without having the right to do so, then God, the Possessor of Might, will ask him about that (deed) on the Day of Resurrection."[2]

77. ʿAbd Allāh b. ʿAmr b. al-ʿĀṣ 🙏 reported that God's Messenger 🙏 said: "Indeed, your body has a right over you; your eyes have a right over you; your wife has a right over you; and your neighbour has a right over you."[3]

78. In another narration, ʿAbd Allāh b. ʿAmr b. al-ʿĀṣ 🙏 related that Allah's Messenger 🙏 said: "The best of companions, in the sight of Allah, is the one who treats his companion best, and the best of neighbours, in the sight of Allah, is the one who treats his neighbour best!"[4]

79. Reported by Burayda b. al-Ḥaṣīb 🙏, God's Messenger 🙏 said: "Stick to the moderate way! Stick to the moderate way! Stick to the moderate way, for no one makes the religion hard on himself save that it will overcome him."[5]

80. According to ʿAbd Allāh b. Masʿūd 🙏, God's Messenger 🙏 said thrice: "The extremists have perished."[6]

---

[1] Set forth by •Muslim in *al-Ṣaḥīḥ*, 3:1548 §1955. •al-Dārimī in *al-Sunan*, 4:123, 125 §17154, 17179.

[2] Set forth by •al-Nasāʾī in *al-Sunan*, 7:206 §4349. •al-Ḥākim in *al-Mustadrak*, 4:261 §7574.

[3] Set forth by •al-Bukhārī in *al-Ṣaḥīḥ*, 2:697 §1874. •Abū Dāwūd in *al-Sunan*, 4:338 §5151–5152.

[4] Set forth by •Aḥmad b. Ḥanbal in *al-Musnad*, 2:167 §6566. •al-Tirmidhī in *al-Sunan*, 4:333 §1944.

[5] Set forth by •Aḥmad b. Ḥanbal in *al-Musnad*, 5:350 §23013. •Ibn Khuzayma in *al-Ṣaḥīḥ*, 2:199 §1179.

[6] Set forth by •Muslim in *al-Ṣaḥīḥ*, 4:2055 §2670. •Aḥmad b. Ḥanbal in *al-Musnad*, 1:386 §3655. •Abū Dāwūd in *al-Sunan*, 4:201 §4608.

81. According to Ibn ʿAbbās ﵄, the Prophet ﷺ narrated from his Lord. He said, "God decreed the good deeds and the bad deeds and explained them. So whoever intends to do a good deed but does not do it, God shall write for him a single complete good deed. If he intends to do a good deed and then does it, God shall write for him ten good deeds, up to seven hundred good deeds, or even multiplied beyond that. And whoever wants to do a bad deed but does not do it, God shall write for him a single good deed. If he intends to do a bad deed and then does it, Allah shall write for him only one bad deed."[1]

82. According to ʿĀʾisha ﵂, God's Messenger ﷺ said: "God loves gentleness in all things."[2]

83. He further said in another narration: "O ʿĀʾisha! God is Gentle and He loves gentleness in all things."[3]

84. According to Jarīr b. ʿAbd Allāh ﵁, the Prophet ﷺ said: "He who is denied gentleness is denied all good."[4]

85. According to ʿAbd Allāh b. ʿUmar ﵄: "One day, a man came to the Prophet ﷺ and submitted: "O Messenger of God! Among all the people, who is dearest to God Most High?" The Messenger of God ﷺ said: 'The one who benefits others the most is dearest to God Most High.' He further said: 'Whoever stops his anger, God Most High will protect his honour; whoever endures his anger, even though he has power, then God Most High will cause his heart to be in bliss on the Day of Resurrection. And whoever walks with his brother to attend to and meet the needs of his brother, then God Most High will keep him

---

[1] Set forth by •al-Bukhārī in *al-Ṣaḥīḥ*, 5:2380 §6126. •Muslim in *al-Ṣaḥīḥ*, 1:118 §131.

[2] Set forth by •al-Bukhārī in *al-Ṣaḥīḥ*, 5:2242 §5678. •Muslim in *al-Ṣaḥīḥ*, 4:1706 §2165.

[3] Set forth by •al-Bukhārī in *al-Ṣaḥīḥ*, 6:2539 §6528. •Ibn Mājah in *al-Sunan*, 2:1216 §3689.

[4] Set forth by •Ibn Abī Shayba in *al-Muṣannaf*, 5:209 §25303.

steadfast on the Day (of Resurrection) when steps would be slipping.'"[1]

86. ʿAbd Allah b. ʿAbbās 🕮 heard the Messenger of God 🕮 saying: "If a Muslim clothes another Muslim, he will remain in the protection of God until a shred of that cloth is left on him."[2]

87. According to ʿUmar b. al-Khaṭṭāb 🕮: "The Messenger of God 🕮 was asked: 'Which deeds are the best?' He said: '(The most excellent deed is) your provision of contentment to a believer by warding off his hunger or clothing him to cover his nakedness or meeting any of his needs.'"[3]

88. According to Abū Hurayra 🕮: "The Messenger of God 🕮 said: 'Whoever grants respite to a deprived one or excuses his loans, God will keep him under the shade of His throne on the Day of Resurrection, when there will be no shade that Day except His shade of mercy.'"[4]

He further said: "He who wants his supplication answered and his troubles removed should make easiness for the deprived (or for a borrower)."[5]

At another occasion, God's Messenger 🕮 said: "Charitable donation does not in any way decrease the wealth, and the servant who forgives, God Most High adds to his honour, and the one who adopts humility for the pleasure of God Most High, Allah elevates his rank."[6]

89. According to ʿAbd Allah b. ʿUmar 🕮: "A man came to the Prophet 🕮 and submitted: 'O Messenger of God! How often shall I forgive a servant?' He gave no reply, so the man repeated what he had said, but he still kept silence.

---

[1] Set forth by •al-Ṭabarānī in *al-Muʿjam al-Awsaṭ*, 6:139–140 §6026.

[2] Set forth by •al-Tirmidhī in *al-Sunan*, 4:651 §2484. •al-Ṭabarānī in *al-Muʿjam al-Kabīr*, 12:97 §12591.

[3] Set forth by •al-Ṭabarānī in *al-Muʿjam al-Awsaṭ*, 5:202 §5081.

[4] Set forth by •al-Tirmidhī in *al-Sunan*, 3:599 §1306.

[5] Set forth by •Muslim in *al-Ṣaḥīḥ*, 3:1196 §1563.

[6] Set forth by •Muslim in *al-Ṣaḥīḥ*, 4:2001 §2588.

When he asked a third time, he replied: 'Forgive him seventy times daily.'"[1]

90. Abū Jurayy al-Hujaymī ⬥ reported: "I submitted to the Messenger of God ⬥: 'We are from villages, teach us an act which, when we perform, God Most High rewards us.' He said: 'Do not despise any good act whether it is pouring water out of your pail to the pail of someone thirsty, and when you talk to your brother have a smile on your face for him.'"[2]

91. The Holy Prophet ⬥ said: "When someone supplicates for his brother in his absence, the angel says: 'May you be credited with the equivalent (of what you have prayed for your brother)!"[3]

And according to ʿAbd Allah b. ʿAbbās ⬥: "God's Messenger ⬥ said: 'Two supplications are such as there is no screen between them and God Most High: a supplication of an oppressed one, and a supplication of a person for his brother in his absence.'"[4]

92. It is narrated that the Holy Prophet ⬥ said: "If someone covers the faults of anyone in this world, God will cover his faults in the Hereafter."[5]

Imam al-Ḥasan al-Baṣrī explained this ḥadīth saying: "It is a betrayal if you disclose your brother's secret."[6]

93. According to ʿUqba b. Āmir ⬥: "The Messenger of God ⬥ said: 'The best excellence is to join the ties with the one

[1] Set forth by •Aḥmad b. Ḥanbal in *al-Musnad*, 2:111 §5899. •Abū Dāwūd in *al-Sunan*, 4:341 §5164.

[2] Set forth by •Ibn Ḥibbān in *al-Ṣaḥīḥ*, 2:281 §522. •al-Ṭabarānī in *al-Muʿjam al-Kabīr*, 7:62 §6383.

[3] Set forth by •Muslim in *al-Ṣaḥīḥ*, 4:2094 §2732.

[4] Set forth by •al-Ṭabarānī in *al-Muʿjam al-Kabīr*, 11:119 §11232.

[5] Set forth by •Muslim in *al-Ṣaḥīḥ*, 4:2002 §2590.

[6] Set forth by •Ibn Abī al-Dunyā in *al-Ṣamt wa Ādāb al-Lisān*, p. 214 §404.

who breaks up with you and grant him who refuses you and overlook the ones who call you bad names.'"[1]

94. According to Abū Bakr ⬥: "On the Day of Resurrection, God Most High will command a herald. Thus, he will proclaim: 'Arise those who have any reward left with God Most High.' Then the people of forgiveness will arise and God Most High will overlook (their faults) in recompense of theirs."[2]

95. According to Abū Mūsā al-Ashʿarī ⬥: "The Prophet ⬥ said, 'Charity is incumbent on every Muslim.' They (the Companions ⬥) submitted, "What if one has nothing (to spend in the way of God)?' He said, 'He should work with his hands (spend his physical and mental energy) so that he may benefit himself and donate to charity.' They submitted, 'What if one does not have (bodily) strength or he cannot do it?' He said, 'Then he should help the helpless and needy (by word or action or both).' They submitted, 'If he is unable to do even that?' He said, 'Then he should enjoin good,' or said, 'he should ordain pious practice.' They said, 'If he could not do that?' He said, 'Then he should refrain from doing anything wrong; that will be considered charity donated by him.'"[3]

96. According to Jābir b. ʿAbd Allāh ⬥: "The Messenger of Allah ⬥ said: 'Every act of righteousness is a charitable donation. Your meeting with your brother with a smiling face, and pouring from your pail into your brother's pail, is also piousness.'"[4]

---

[1] Set forth by •Aḥmad b. Ḥanbal in *al-Musnad*, 4:158 §17488.

[2] Set forth by •al-Marwazī in *Musnad Abī Bakr*, p. 73 §21. •Aḥmad b. Ḥanbal in *Faḍāʾil al-Ṣaḥāba*, 1:439 §700.

[3] Set forth by •al-Bukhārī in *al-Ṣaḥīḥ*, 5:2241 §5676. •Muslim in *al-Ṣaḥīḥ*, 2:699 §1008.

[4] Set forth by •Aḥmad b. Ḥanbal in *al-Musnad*, 3:360 §14920. •al-Tirmidhī in *al-Sunan*, 4:347 §1970.

97. And according to Abū Dharr ﷺ: "God's Messenger ﷺ said: 'Your smiling in your brother's face is a charity to your credit. Your enjoining what is right and forbidding what is wrong is a charitable donation to your credit. Your guiding the man who has lost his way is a charitable donation to your credit. Your leading the poor-sighted man to his path is a charitable donation to your credit. Your clearing the stone, the thorn and the bone from the path is also a charitable donation to your credit. Your pouring from your pail into your brother's pail is a charitable donation to your credit.'"[1]

98. According to Anas b. Mālik ﷺ: "God's Messenger ﷺ said: 'Charity surely cools the wrath of the Lord and wards off an evil death.'"[2]

99. According to Maymūna, the daughter of Saʿd ﷺ: "I submitted: 'O God's Messenger! Inform us about charity.' He said: 'Whoever gives to charity with the intention to seek the reward and the pleasure of God Most High, it barricades him from Hellfire.'"[3]

100. According to Rāfiʿ b. Khadīj ﷺ: "The Messenger of God ﷺ said: 'The charity locks seventy doors of evil.'"[4]

101. And in a tradition, Abū Hurayra ﷺ narrated: "The Messenger of God ﷺ said: 'Indeed, (firstly) one of the virtuous deeds for which reward continues reaching a believer after his death is the knowledge that he teaches and disseminates; (secondly) the pious son, his successor; (thirdly) the copy of the Qurʾān that he bequeaths; (fourthly) the mosque that he erects; (fifthly) the inn he builds for wayfarers; (sixthly) the waterway that he brings about and commissions; (and seventhly) the alms he gives

---

[1] Set forth by •al-Tirmidhī in *al-Sunan*, 4:339 §1956.

[2] Set forth by •al-Tirmidhī in *al-Sunan*, 3:52 §664. •Ibn Ḥibbān in *al-Ṣaḥīḥ*, 8:103 §3309.

[3] Set forth by •al-Ṭabarānī in *al-Muʿjam al-Kabīr*, 25:35 §62.

[4] Set forth by •al-Ṭabarānī in *al-Muʿjam al-Kabīr*, 4:274 §4402.

away from his wealth during his lifetime in fine fettle. The reward of all these pious acts continues reaching him after his death as well.'"[1]

102. According to Muʿādh b. Anas ☙, the Prophet ﷺ said: "Whoever teaches knowledge will get the reward of the one who practises it, without any deduction from his (the doer's) reward."[2]

103. According to Abū al-Dardāʾ ☙: "The Messenger of God ﷺ said: 'Shall I not inform you of something more excellent in degree than fasting, prayer and alms-due (Zakāt)? The people submitted: 'Yes.' He said: 'The act of reconciliation amongst people, while creating discord amongst them eliminates safety.'"[3]

104. According to ʿAbd Allāh b. ʿAmr ☙: "The Messenger of God ﷺ said: 'The best charity is to bring reconciliation between two close relatives."[4]

105. According to Abū Umāma ☙: "The Messenger of God ﷺ said to Abū Ayyūb b. Zayd: 'Shall I not inform you about an act that pleases God and His Prophet?' He submitted: 'Why not, O Messenger of God!' He said: 'When people fight, bring reconciliation amongst them and when distance occurs, create nearness amongst them."[5]

106. HIS ACTS OF REMEMBRANCE

(1) When he encountered something pleasing to him, he said: "Praise is due to God through whose grace good tidings are brought to earth." When he encountered something unpleasant, he said: "Praise is due to God under all

---

[1] Set forth by •Ibn Mājah in *al-Sunan*, 1:88 §242.

[2] Set forth by •Ibn Mājah in *al-Sunan*, 1:88 §240. •al-Ṭabarānī in *al-Muʿjam al-Kabīr*, 20:198 §446.

[3] Set forth by •Aḥmad b. Ḥanbal in *al-Musnad*, 6:444 §27548. •Abū Dāwūd in *al-Sunan*, 4:280 §4919.

[4] Set forth by •al-Quḍāʿī in *Musnad al-Shihāb*, 2:244 §1280. •ʿAbd b. Ḥumayd in *al-Musnad*, 1:135 §335.

[5] Set forth by •al-Ṭabarānī in *al-Muʿjam al-Kabīr*, 8:257 §7999.

circumstances."[1] When he swore an oath, he often said: "By Him who holds the life of Abū al-Qāsim in His hands."[2]

(2) When he would lie down to sleep, he would put his hand under his cheek and say: "In Your name, O God, I live and in Your name I die."[3] When he used to go to bed, he would say: "In the name of God I lie down upon my side. O God, forgive my sins, and drive away my personal devil. Redeem my pledge and make my good deeds weigh heavy in the scale and set me in the Highest Assembly."[4]

(3) When he sent someone to work and fight for God's sake, he would say: "Unto God I commend your religion, your trust, and the completion of your work."[5]

(4) On starting a trip he would say: "O God, with You I go to battle, with You I depart, and with You I travel."[6]

(5) When he prayed for rain, he said: "O God, give Your servants drink, shower all with Your mercy and bring to life Your dead land," and "O God, bestow blessings, adornments and dwellings in this land, and provide our sustenance, You are the best of sustainers."[7]

(6) When the north wind blew hard, he would say: "O God, I seek refuge in You from the evil that has befallen."[8]

(7) When he was saddened, he would say: "The Lord is not in need of worship. The Creator is not in need of the creation. The Sustainer is not in need of the sustained. Sufficient unto me is He Who is sufficient unto me. God is sufficient unto

---

[1] Set forth by •Ibn Mājah in *al-Sunan*, 2:1250 §3803.

[2] Set forth by •Aḥmad b. Ḥanbal in *al-Musnad*, 3:48 §11462. •Abū Dāwūd in *al-Sunan*, 3:225 §3264.

[3] Set forth by •al-Bukhārī in *al-Ṣaḥīḥ*, 5:2327 §5955.

[4] Set forth by •al-Bukhārī in *al-Ṣaḥīḥ*, 6:2691 §6958.

[5] Set forth by •Abū Dāwūd in *al-Sunan*, 3:34 §2600–2601. •al-Tirmidhī in *al-Sunan*, 5:499 §3442–3443.

[6] Set forth by •Aḥmad b. Ḥanbal in *al-Musnad*, 1:150 §1295.

[7] Set forth by •Abū Dāwūd in *al-Sunan*, 1:305 §1176.

[8] Set forth by •Abū Dāwūd in *al-Sunan*, 4:326 §5099.

me, and how excellent a guardian is He! God is sufficient unto me; there is not god but He. On Him I rely, and He is the Lord of the glorious throne."[1]

(8) Every morning and every evening he prayed: "O God, I ask You to surprise me with good tidings, and I seek refuge in You from sudden evil, for the servant has no knowledge of what may unexpectedly occur in the morning or the evening."[2]

(9) As he woke up in the mornings and as the sun set he would say: "We entered upon the morning as followers of the religion of Islam, of the doctrine of the Oneness of God, of the religion of our Prophet Muhammad ﷺ, and of the creed of our father Abraham, who was upright and was not among those who set equals to God."[3]

(10) When he broke his fast, he would say: "My Lord, it is for Your sake that I fasted, and with Your sustenance did I break the fast. Accept this fast from me; You are the All-Hearing, the All-Knowing,"[4] and "Praise be to God Who aided me to fast and provided me with sustenance that I might break the fast."[5] When he broke fast in someone's house, he would say: "A fasting person has broken his fast in your home, and thus, the angels have invoked blessings upon you."[6]

---

[1] Set forth by •al-Suyūṭī in *Shamā'il al-Sharīfa*, p. 90 §111. •al-Hindī in *Kanz al-ʿUmmāl*, 7:28 §18009.

[2] Set forth by •Ibn al-Sunnī in *ʿAmal al-Yawm wa al-Layla*, p. 40 §39.

[3] Set forth by •Aḥmad b. Ḥanbal in *al-Musnad*, 3:406 §153979. •al-Nasā'ī in *al-Sunan al-Kubrā*, 6:3 §9829.

[4] Set forth by •al-Ṭabarānī in *al-Muʿjam al-Kabīr*, 12:146 §12720.

[5] Set forth by •Ibn Abī Shayba in *al-Muṣannaf*, 2:344 §9744.

[6] Set forth by •Aḥmad b. Ḥanbal in *al-Musnad*, 3:201 §13108. •Abū Dāwūd in *al-Sunan*, 3:367 §3854.

(11) When he ate or he drank he said: 'Praise be to God Who fed us and gave us to drink, made it agreeable to swallow and made an outlet."[1]

(12) As he entered his room, he would say: "Praise be to God, Who gave us food and drink, provided us sufficiently and gave us shelter. How many there are who have neither provider nor shelter!"[2]

(13) As he turned from one side to another in his bed, he would say: "There is no god but God, the One, the Ever-Dominant, the Lord of the heavens and the earth and whatever is between them, the Victorious, the All-Forgiving.".[3]

(14) When some matter bothered him, he said: "There is no god but God, the Clement, the Generous. Glory be to God, the Lord of the glorious throne. Praise be to God, the Lord of the universe."[4]

(15) When he expected harm to come from his enemies, he would pray: "O God, we place You in front of them and seek refuge in You from their mischief."[5]

(16) When he suspected a mischief directed against him, he would pray: "O God bestow Your blessings on this and do not cause it harm."[6]

(17) When he left his house, he would pray: "In the name of God. Reliance is on God. There is no power nor strength save in God."[7] Or he would pray: "In the name of God. Upon God I rely. O God, we seek refuge in You lest we

---

[1] Set forth by •Abū Dāwūd in *al-Sunan*, 3:366 §3851.

[2] Set forth by •Muslim in *al-Ṣaḥīḥ*, 4:2085 §2715.

[3] Set forth by •al-Nasāʾī in *al-Sunan al-Kubrā*, 6:216 §10700. •Ibn Ḥibbān in *al-Ṣaḥīḥ*, 12:340 §5530.

[4] Set forth by •al-Bukhārī in *al-Ṣaḥīḥ*, 5:2336 §5986. •al-Tirmidhī in *al-Sunan*, 2:344 §479.

[5] Set forth by •Aḥmad b. Ḥanbal in *al-Musnad*, 4:414 §19735.

[6] Set forth by •Ibn al-Sunnī in *ʿAmal al-Yawm wa al-Layla*, 1:171 §208. •al-Suyūṭī in *al-Shamāʾil al-Sharīfa*, p. 123 §178.

[7] Set forth by •Abū Dāwūd in *al-Sunan*, 4:325 §5095.

slip, or wrong or be wronged, or act foolishly, or any one act foolishly with us."[1] Or he would pray: "In the name of God. My Lord, I seek refuge in Thee lest I slip, or lead someone astray, or wrong or be wronged, or act foolishly, or any one act foolishly with me."[2] Or he would pray: "In the name of God. I rely upon God. There is no power nor strength, save in God. O God, I seek refuge in You lest I send any one astray, or go astray myself, or slip or cause someone else to slip, or wrong or be wronged, or act foolishly, or anyone act foolishly with me, or oppress or be oppressed."[3]

(18) When he entered a mosque,: "I seek refuge in God the Magnificent, in His glorious Self, and in His eternal Dominion from the accursed Devil.".[4]

(19) Sometimes upon entering a mosque,: "In the name of God, Peace be upon the Messenger of God. O God, forgive me my sins and open unto me the gates of Your mercy."[5] Sometimes he prayed: "In the name of God. Peace be upon the Messenger of God. O God, forgive me my sins and open unto me the gates of Your grace and favour."[6] Alternatively, he would say: "My Lord, forgive me my sins and open unto me the gates of Your mercy."[7] Or he would say: "My Lord, forgive me my sins and open unto me the gates of Your grace and favor."[8] Or he would say: "In the

---

[1] Set forth by •Aḥmad b. Ḥanbal in *al-Musnad*, 6:306 §26658.

[2] Set forth by •al-Nasāʾī in *al-Sunan*, 8:285 §5539.

[3] Set forth by •al-Suyūṭī in *al-Shamāʾil al-Sharīfa*, p. 127 §186. •al-Hindī in *Kanz al-ʿUmmāl*, 7:54 §18420.

[4] Set forth by •Abū Dāwūd in *al-Sunan*, 1:127 §466.

[5] Set forth by •Aḥmad b. Ḥanbal in *al-Musnad*, 6:283 §26460. •Ibn Mājah in *al-Sunan*, 1:253 §771.

[6] Ibid.

[7] Set forth by •al-Tirmidhī in *al-Sunan*, 2:127 §314.

[8] Ibid.

name of God. My Lord, blessings be upon Muhammad and the family of Muhammad."[1]

(20) When he went to relieve himself, he would say: "In the name of God. I seek refuge from obstruction and whatever gets obstructed."[2]

Or else he would say: "Praise be to God who made me appreciate this matter, who provided me with strength, and who removed its unpleasantness from me."[3]

(21) When he left the privy, he would say: 'Your pardon,"[4] or "Praise be to God Who relieved me from suffering and gave me health"[5] or: "Praise be to God in the beginning of the matter and in its end."[6]

(22) When he entered a marketplace he would pray: "In the name of God. O God, I ask of You the good of this market, and the good of that which is therein; and I seek refuge in You from the evil thereof, and the evil of that which is therein. O God, I seek refuge in You lest I strike a bargain herein incurring a lost or meet with a false oath."[7]

(23) When he visited graveyards, he addressed the graves: "Peace be upon you, O mortal souls with decayed flesh and rotten bones, who departed this world believing in God. O God, impart upon them a spirit from You and peace from us."[8]

---

[1] Set forth by •al-Suyūṭī in *al-Shamā'il al-Sharīfa*, p. 138 §203. •al-Hindī in *Kanz al-ʿUmmāl*, 7:25 §17964.

[2] Set forth by •al-Bukhārī in *al-Ṣaḥīḥ*, 1:66 §142.

[3] Set forth by •Ibn Mājah in *al-Sunan*, 1:110 §301.

[4] Set forth by •al-Tirmidhī in *al-Sunan*, 1:12 §7.

[5] Set forth by •Ibn Mājah in *al-Sunan*, 1:110 §301.

[6] Set forth by •al-Suyūṭī in *al-Shamā'il al-Sharīfa*, p. 125 §181. •al-Hindī in *Kanz al-ʿUmmāl*, 7:20 §17871.

[7] Set forth by •al-Ḥākim in *al-Mustadrak*, 1:723 §1977.

[8] Set forth by •Ibn al-Sunnī in *ʿAmal al-Yawm wa al-Layla*, p. 545 §593. •al-Hindī in *Kanz al-ʿUmmāl*, 7:60 §18517.

(24) When it rained, he prayed: "O God, make it a profitable downpour."[1]

(25) When he saw the new moon he prayed: "O God, let this new moon appear unto us with peace and faith, with safety and Islam. My Lord and your Lord is God.".[2]

Or he would pray: "O God, I ask You to bestow upon us all that is good of this month, and I seek refuge in You from the misfortunes of destiny and the misfortunes of the Day of Judgment."[3]

(26) May the new month be a source of good: "O God, let this new moon be a moon of prosperity and guidance.[4]

(27) When something annoyed him, he would say: "God, God is my Sustainer. He has no partner."[5]

(28) He congratulated newly married men, saying: "May God bless you and happily unite the two of you."[6]

(29) He would often raise his eyes to heaven and say: "O Director of hearts, keep my heart in a state of obedience to You."[7]

(30) When he saw lightning or heard thunder he said: "O God, slay us not with Your wrath, and destroy us not with Your punishment, but preserve us before that."[8]

(31) When he drank, he said: "Praise be to God who quenched our thirst through His mercy, with fresh sweet water. Praise be to Him for not making it salty with our sins."[9]

---

[1] Set forth by •al-Bukhārī in *al-Ṣaḥīḥ*, 1:349 §985.

[2] Set forth by •Aḥmad b. Ḥanbal in *al-Musnad*, 1:162 §1397. •al-Tirmidhī in *al-Sunan*, 5:504 §3451.

[3] Set forth by •Ibn Abī Shayba in *al-Muṣannaf*, 2:342 §9727.

[4] Set forth by •Abū Dāwūd in *al-Sunan*, 4:324 §5092.

[5] Set forth by •al-Nasāʾī in *al-Sunan al-Kubrā*, 6:168 §10493.

[6] Set forth by •Abū Dāwūd in *al-Sunan*, 2:241 §2130.

[7] Set forth by •Aḥmad b. Ḥanbal in *al-Musnad*, 2:418 §9410.

[8] Set forth by •Aḥmad b. Ḥanbal in *al-Musnad*, 2:100 §5763.

[9] Set forth by •al-Ṭabarānī in *al-Duʿāʾ*, p. 280 §899. •Abū Nuʿaym in *Ḥilya al-Awliyāʾ*, 8:137.

(32) When a storm was brewing, he would pray: "O God, I beg of You the good of this, and the good of that which has been sent therewith. I seek refuge in You from the evil of this and the evil of that which has been sent therewith."[1]

(33) When he sneezed, he said: "Praise be to God." When those around him responded: "May God have mercy on you," he would reply: "May God guide you and make you righteous."[2]

(34) After meals he would pray: "Praise be to God who fed us and gave us drink and made us Muslims; O God, praise be to You. You fed us satisfying our hunger, gave us to drink quenching our thirst. Therefore, unceasing, never-parting, indispensable praise be to You."[3]

Or he would pray: "O God, You fed us and gave us to drink. You bestowed riches upon us and guided us. O God, all praise belongs to You for what You have given and chosen."[4]

(35) Bowing and prostrating, he would say: "Glory be to You. All praise be to You. I seek Your forgiveness and I turn unto You in repentance."[5]

(36) When he looked into a mirror he would say: "Praise be to God Who has formed my person well, made it symmetric, fashioned it into my figure, finished it well, and set me among the Muslims."[6]

---

[1] Set forth by •Muslim in *al-Ṣaḥīḥ*, 2:616 §899.

[2] Set forth by •al-Bukhārī in *al-Ṣaḥīḥ*, 5:2298 §5870.

[3] Set forth by •Aḥmad b. Ḥanbal in *al-Musnad*, 4:236 §18096. •al-Ṭabarānī in *al-Muʿjam al-Kabīr*, 3:268 §3372.

[4] Set forth by •Aḥmad b. Ḥanbal in *al-Musnad*, 4:62 §16646. •al-Nasāʾī in *al-Sunan al-Kubrā*, 4:202 §6898. •al-Sunnī in *ʿAmal al-Yawm wa al-Layla*, p. 416 §465.

[5] Set forth by •al-Bazzār in *al-Musnad*, 5:343–344 §1970. •al-Ṭabarānī in *al-Muʿjam al-Kabīr*, 10:155 §10302.

[6] Set forth by •al-Ṭabarānī in *al-Muʿjam al-Awsaṭ*, 1:240 §787. •al-Sunnī in *ʿAmal al-Yawm wa al-Layla*, p. 139 §165. •al-Bayhaqī in *Shuʿab*

(37) When the wind blew, he turned toward it and said: "O God, we beg of You the good of this wind, and the good of that which has been sent therewith. And I seek refuge in You from the evil thereof, and the evil of that which is therein. O God let this wind be a merciful blessing, and let it not be a punishment. O God, let it be a blessed wind and let it not be an accursed wind."[1]

107. HIS PASSING: He left this world at the age of 63, in the city of Medina, to which he had migrated ten years earlier. His last words were: "The sublime majesty of my Lord! For I have fulfilled my mission,"[2] and then he gave up his blessed soul.

His last advice to us was: "Do not ever abandon prayer. Do not ever abandon prayer. Do not ever abandon prayer. And fear God in your treatment of those under your control."[3]

108. One day, during the caliphate of ʿUmar ﷺ, while he was sitting with his companions, three noble and beautiful young men entered his presence. Two of them said, "We two are brothers. While our father was working in his field, he was killed by this young man, whom we have brought to you for justice. Punish him according to God's Book.» The caliph turned to the third young man and asked him to speak.

"Although there were no witnesses, God, the Ever-Present, knows they are telling the truth," said the accused. "I regret very much that their father found death at my

---

al-Īmān, 4:111 §4458.

[1] Set forth by •al-Ṭabarānī in *al-Muʿjam al-Kabīr*, 11:213 §11533. •Abū Yaʿlā in *al-Musnad*, 4:341 §2456. •al-Haythamī in *Majmaʿ al-Zawāʾid*, 10:135.

[2] Set forth by •al-Ḥākim in *al-Mustadrak*, 3:58 §4387. •al-Suyūṭī in *al-Shamāʾil al-Sharīfa*, p.376 §722.

[3] Set forth by •Khaṭīb Baghdādī in *Tārīkh Baghdād*, 10:169 §5307. •al-Hindī in *Kanz al-ʿUmmāl*, 7:113 §18864.

hands. I am a villager. I arrived in Medina this morning to visit the tomb of our Prophet ﷺ. At the outskirts of the city, I got off my horse to take ablution. My horse started eating from the branch of a date tree that was hanging over a wall. As soon as I noticed this, I pulled my horse away from the branch." At that moment an angry old man approached with a big stone in his hand. He threw the stone at my horse's head, killing it instantly. Since I loved my horse very much, I lost control of myself. I picked up the stone and threw it back at the man. He fell dead. If I had wanted to escape, I could have done so, but where? If I do not meet my punishment here, I shall meet an eternal punishment in the hereafter. I had not intended to kill this man, but he died by my hand. Now the judgment is yours."

The caliph said, "You have committed murder. According to Islamic law, you must receive treatment equal to that which you have dispensed."

Although this was a pronouncement of death, the young man kept his composure and calmly said, "So be it. However, a fortune has been left in my care to be given to an orphan when he comes of age. I buried this fortune for safekeeping. Nobody knows where it is but me. I must dig it up and leave it in somebody else's care; otherwise the orphan will be denied his right. Give me three days to go to my village and attend to this duty."

ʿUmar ﵁ replied, "Your request cannot be accorded unless somebody takes your place and vouches for your life."

"O Ruler of the Faithful," said the young man, "I could have escaped before if I had wished. My heart is filled with the fear of God; be certain I will be back."

The caliph refused on the basis of the Law. The young man looked at the noble Companions ﵃ of the Prophet ﷺ who were gathered around the caliph. Choosing at random, he pointed to Abū Dharr al-Ghifārī ﵁ and said,

"This man will be the one to vouch for me." Abū Dharr g was one of the most beloved and respected Companions ﵇ of the Prophet ﷺ. Without hesitation he agreed to replace the young man.

The accused was released. On the third day, the two young accusers came back to the caliph's court. Abū Dharr ﵁ was there, but not the accused. The accusers said, "O Abū Dharr, you vouched for someone you did not know. Even if he does not return, we will not leave without receiving the price of our father›s blood."

The caliph said, "Indeed, if the young man does not return, we will have to apply his punishment to Abū Dharr." Hearing this, everyone present began to weep, for Abū Dharr, a man of perfect virtue and splendid character, was the light and inspiration for all of Medina.

When the third day had come to an end, the excitement, sorrow and amazement of the people reached their peak. Suddenly the young man appeared. He had been running and was tired, dusty and hot. "I am sorry to have worried you," he said breathlessly. "Pardon me for arriving at the last minute. There was much work to be done, the desert is hot, and the trip was long. I am now ready; execute my punishment."

Then he turned to the crowd and said, "The man of faith is loyal to his word. The one who fails to keep his word is a hypocrite. Who can escape death, which comes sooner or later anyway? Did you think I was going to disappear and make people say, 'The Muslims do not keep their word anymore'?"

The crowd then turned to Abū Dharr ﵁ and asked whether he had known of the young man's fine character. He answered, "Not at all, but I did not feel that I could refuse him when he singled me out, as it would not have been in keeping with the laws of generosity. Should I be the one to make people say that there is no more kindness left in Islam?"

The hearts of the accusers trembled, and they dropped their claim, saying, "Should we be the ones to make people say that there is no more compassion left in Islam?"[1]

109. ʿAlī 🕮, the last of the divinely guided caliphs, the Lion of God, the symbol of knowledge, generosity, and loyalty, the father of the grandchildren of the Prophet 🕮, was also known as the invincible warrior of his time. In one battle he had overpowered an enemy warrior and had his dagger at the man›s throat when the nonbeliever spat in his face. Immediately ʿAlī 🕮 got up, sheathed his dagger, and told the man, "Taking your life is unlawful to me. Go away!" The man, who had saved his life by spitting in the face of the revered Lion of God, was amazed. "O ʿAlī," he asked, "I was helpless, you were about to kill me, I insulted you and you released me. Why?" "When you spat in my face," ʿAlī 🕮 answered, "It aroused the anger of my ego. Had I killed you then it would not have been for the sake of God, but for the sake of my ego. I would have been a murderer. You are free to go." The enemy warrior, moved by the integrity displayed in ʿAlī, converted to Islam on the spot.[2]

110. ʿAbd Allāh b. Masʿūd 🕮 related: "The Prophet of God 🕮 said: 'Truly, God provided me with the best rules of conduct and perfected my adab. Then, He ordered me to uphold noble traits of character, by His words: ﴾(O Esteemed Beloved!) Adopt forbearance, always command piousness, and keep aloof from the ignorant.﴿ [Q.7:199].'"[3]

---

[1] Set forth by •al-Itlīdī in *Nawādir al-Khulafāʾ* generally known as *Iʿlām al-Nās bimā Waqaʿa liʾl-Barāmika maʿ Banī al-ʿAbbās*, p. 11. •Luʾīs Shaykhū al-Yasūʿī in *Majānī al-Adab fī Ḥadāʾiq al-ʿArab*, 4:230.

[2] Set forth by •al-Mullā ʿAlī al-Qārī in *Mirqāt al-Mafātīḥ sharḥ Mishkāt al-Maṣābīḥ*, 7:10.

[3] Set forth by •al-Samʿānī in *Adab al-Imlāʾ waʾl-Istimlāʾ*, p. 1. •al-Sakhāwī in *al-Maqāṣid al-Ḥasana*, 1:73 §45. •al-Munāwī in *Fayḍ al-Qadīr*, 1:225.

Part II

63 Specific Descriptions Outlining the True Image of the Personality of the Holy Prophet Muhammad ﷺ

I

The Most Noble of Lineage

The Prophet Muhammad ﷺ was born in a modest family of noble lineage. He ﷺ was a descendant of Prophet Abraham ﷺ and was from the best tribes of the Arabs, which was the tribe of Quraysh. From within the Quraysh, he ﷺ came from the most noble of the families known as the clan of Hāshim. His grandfather ʿAbd al-Muṭṭalib ﷺ was the custodian of the Kaʿba and the chief of Mecca. Thus, he came from a noble lineage from a highly respected and honourable family.

Informing his Companions ﷺ about his family background, the Prophet Muhammad ﷺ said, "'I am Muhammad b. ʿAbd Allāh b. ʿAbd al-Muṭṭalib. Indeed, God created the creation, and He put me in the best group of them, then He made them into two groups, so He put me in the best group of them, then He made them into tribes, so He put me in the best of tribes, then He made them into houses, so He put me in the best of them in tribe and lineage.'[1]

[1] Set forth by •Aḥmad b. Ḥanbal in *al-Musnad*, 1:210 §1788. •al-Tirmidhī in *al-Sunan*, 5:543, 584 §§§3532, 3607–3608.

2

The Embodiment of Beauty

The Companions ﷺ of the Prophet ﷺ had preserved a description of the physical beauty of Prophet Muhammad ﷺ. They said that he ﷺ was the most excellent of countenance with the finest of character.[1] They agreed that there was none more beautiful than him ﷺ.[2]

Concerning his physical appearance, they said that he ﷺ had a bright appearance as though he was made from light[3] and that his teeth would glisten like they were pearls.[4] He was neither too tall nor short but was slightly taller than medium height and his body was perfectly proportioned.[5] His face was neither long, nor round, but in between the two.[6] His skin was as soft as silk[7] and he ﷺ had a beautiful fragrance like that of musk.[8]

---

[1] Set forth by •al-Bukhārī in *al-Ṣaḥīḥ*, 3:1303 §3356. •Muslim in *al-Ṣaḥīḥ*, 4:1819 §2337.

[2] Set forth by •al-Bukhārī in *al-Ṣaḥīḥ*, 3:1303 §3358. •Muslim in *al-Ṣaḥīḥ*, 4:1818 §2337.

[3] Set forth by •al-Dārimī in *al-Sunan*, 1:44 §57.

[4] Set forth by •al-Tirmidhī in *al-Shamāʾil al-Muḥammadiyya*, pp. 36–38 §8. •al-Ṭabarānī in *al-Muʿjam al-Kabīr*, 22:155–156.

[5] Set forth by •al-Tirmidhī in *al-Sunan*, 5:599 §3638.

[6] Set forth by •al-Bayjūrī in *al-Muwāhib al-Laduniyya ʿalā al-Shamāʾil al-Muhammadiyya*, p. 25.

[7] Set forth by •al-Bukhārī in *al-Ṣaḥīḥ*, 2:696 §1872.

[8] Set forth by •al-Bukhārī in *al-Ṣaḥīḥ*, 2:696 §1872.

The Prophet's hair was black in colour,[1] and it was neither curly nor straight but moderately wavy.[2] His hair was long, and it reached the bottom of his ear or up to his shoulders.[3] At the time of his passing, which was 63 years in age, the Prophet ﷺ had only a few strands of white hair, which according to some narrations was not more than 14 strands of hair.[4] His forehead was broad,[5] and his eyebrows were thin.[6] When he spoke, a light could be seen shining from his blessed mouth as though he was made from light.[7]

---

1 Set forth by •Maʿmar b. Rāshid in *al-Jāmiʿ*, 11:259 §20490.

2 Set forth by •al-Bukhārī in *al-Ṣaḥīḥ*, 5:2212 §5566. •Muslim in *al-Ṣaḥīḥ*, 4:1819 §2338.

3 Set forth by •al-Bukhārī in *al-Ṣaḥīḥ*, 5:2211 §5561. •Muslim in *al-Ṣaḥīḥ*, 4:1818 §2337.

4 Set forth by •Aḥmad b. Ḥanbal in *al-Musnad*, 3:165 §12713. •ʿAbd al-Razzāq in *al-Muṣannaf*, 11:155 §20185.

5 Set forth by •al-Tirmidhī in *al-Shamāʾil al-Muḥammadiyya*, p. 37 §8. •Ibn Ḥibbān in *al-Thiqāt*, 2:145–146.

6 Set forth by •Abū Yaʿlā in *al-Musnad*, 12:213 §6830.

7 Set forth by •al-Dārimī in *al-Sunan*, 1:44 §58. •al-Tirmidhī in *al-Shamāʾil al-Muḥammadiyya*, p. 41 §15.

3

The Possessor of Excellent Names and Titles

Prophet Muhammad ﷺ had many excellent names and titles. His name 'Muhammad' means 'the Praised One'.[1] This name was not common amongst the Arabs before him.[2] However, it is amongst the most common names in the world today with approximately 150 million people in the world bearing this name with all its different variations in spelling.

Before announcing his Prophethood, Prophet Muhammad ﷺ was known as '*al-Amīn*', which means 'the Honest'.[3] This title was given to him by his society because he was known for his truthfulness and integrity. Likewise, before he was sent as God's Prophet, the Prophets of former communities, such as Prophets Moses and Jesus, had given glad tidings of his coming. They would refer to him by the name '*Aḥmad*', which means the 'Most Praised'.[4] This name is from the same root as the name 'Muhammad'.

The Prophet Muhammad ﷺ whilst discussing with his Companions about the different titles given to the Prophets said that he was conferred the title 'Ḥabīb Allāh', which means the 'Beloved of God'.[5] In the Holy Bible, he is given

1 Set forth by •al-Rāghib al-Aṣfahānī in *al-Mufradāt*, p. 131.

2 Set forth by •al-Qusṭulānī in *al-Mawāhib al-Laduniyya*, 2:38.

3 Set forth by •al-Qurṭubī in *al-Jāmiʿ li-Aḥkām al-Qurʾān*, 6:416.

4 Qurʾān 61:6.

5 Set forth by •al-Tirmidhī in *al-Sunan*, 5:587 §3616. •al-Dārimī in *al-Sunan*, 1:42 §54.

the title of the 'Paraclete' which means the 'Intercessor'.[1] The Prophet ﷺ is also given this title in Arabic, which is the word '*al-Shafīʿ*'.[2] This title is given to him because Prophet Muhammad ﷺ will intercede for humanity and seek forgiveness for the sinners and pray for them to be freed from the Hellfire.

[1] Set forth by •Qāḍī ʿIyāḍ in *al-Shifāʾ*, 1:321. •al-Qusṭulānī in *al-Mawāhib al-Laduniyya*, 2:53. •al-Suyūṭī in *al-Riyāḍ al-Anīqa fī Sharḥ Asmāʾ Khayr al-Khalīqa*, p. 129.

[2] Set forth by •al-Tirmidhī in *al-Sunan*, 5:587 §3616. •al-Dārimī in *al-Sunan*, 1:39, 42 §47, 54.

4

The One with the Highest Moral Character

"I have been sent to perfect excellent moral character," the Prophet Muhammad ﷺ said. Showing good character and excellent moral behaviour was extremely important to the beloved Prophet of God ﷺ. His whole life was a practical demonstration of good character and excellent morals. God praised him in the Qurʾān saying: ﴾*In truth, in (the sacred person of) God's Messenger (Muhammad), there is for you a most perfect and beautiful model for every such person that expects and aspires to (meet) God and the Last Day and remembers God abundantly.*﴿ [Q.33:21.]

Such is the importance of good character and morals that the Prophet Muhammad ﷺ said: "Indeed the most beloved among you to me, and the nearest to sit with me on the Day of Judgment is the best of you in character. And indeed, the most disliked among you to me, and the one sitting farthest from me on the Day of Judgement ... is the arrogant."[1]

[1] Set forth by •Aḥmad b. Ḥanbal in *al-Musnad*, 2:185 §6735. •al-Tirmidhī in *al-Sunan*, 4:370 §2018.

5

The Most Humble

The beloved Prophet of God ﷺ was humble and he loved humbleness and humility. He ﷺ disliked pride and arrogance. From his humility,[1] he ﷺ would sit on the floor, eat sitting on the ground and accept the invitations of slaves and eat the food that they ate. He ﷺ would partake in the household chores with his family and would sit with the poor and weak. He ﷺ taught others to humble themselves and not to feel superiority over others, as the one who thinks he is superior to others will be brought down by God.[2]

[1] Set forth by •Muslim in *al-Ṣaḥīḥ*, 4:2198 §2865.

[2] Set forth by •al-Bukhārī in *al-Ṣaḥīḥ*, 5:2255 §5724. •al-Tirmidhī in *al-Sunan*, 3:337 §1017. •al-Ṭabarānī in *al-Muʿjam al-Kabīr*, 12:67 §12494. •al-Bayhaqī in *Shuʿab al-Īmān*, 6:290 §8192.

6

The Most Truthful and Honest

Abū Sufyān ﷺ was amongst the Meccans who embraced Islam towards the end of the Prophet's life. For most part of 23 years, he had opposed Islam and had waged bitter wars against the Prophet ﷺ. Once before becoming a Muslim, he went onto a business trip to Syria. He found himself at the court of Heraclius, who asked him about the Prophet Muhammad ﷺ. Heraclius asked: "Have you ever accused him of telling lies before his claim (to be a Prophet)?" Abū Sufyān replied, "No." Heraclius then asked: "Does he break his promises?" And Abū Sufyān replied, "No."

Commenting on Abū Sufyān's reply, Heraclius said: "If he does not lie to people, then certainly he will not lie about God... such is the practice of the Prophets that they do not deceive others." In fact, the Prophet ﷺ was known for his truthfulness and honesty among his people that even his most bitter enemies would entrust their valuables and belongings to him as they knew that there was no one more truthful and trustworthy than him. The Jewish Rabbi ʿAbd Allāh b. Salām, when he first saw the Prophet ﷺ, noted: "When I looked at the face of the Messenger of God, I realised that his face was not the face of a liar."[1]

[1] Set forth by •al-Bukhārī in *al-Ṣaḥīḥ*, 1:7–8 §7. •Muslim in *al-Ṣaḥīḥ*, 3:1393–1395 §1773.

7

The Most Just and Fair

The Prophet Muhammad ﷺ treated people fairly. He did not allow Muslims to oppress non-Muslims and get away with it. He ﷺ said: "If a Muslim kills a Christian, he will be killed (in retaliation)."[1]

On another occasion, a woman from the powerful tribes of Mecca was found guilty of stealing. So, the Holy Prophet ﷺ passed judgement that she would be punished. However, some of the Companions tried to plead with the Prophet ﷺ not to punish her because she came from a rich family. But the Prophet ﷺ instead got up and addressed his Companions, saying: "Those before were destroyed because when the elites among them stole (i.e. committed a crime), they would let them off, but if some poor person stole they would punish him (for his crime). By God, if Fāṭima, the daughter of Muhammad, stole, I would cut her hand also (i.e. punish her for her crime)."[2]

From this anecdote we can see the principle of equality before the law that no one is above the law. The Prophet's justice and fairness was so great that he would not allow the elite to get away with their crimes and punish only the common people. He ﷺ declared that even his own family must abide by the law and not contravene it.

---

[1] Set forth by •al-Shāfiʿī in *al-Musnad*, p. 343. •al-Bayhaqī in *al-Sunan al-Kubrā*, 8:30 §15696.

[2] Set forth by al-Bukhārī in *al-Ṣaḥīḥ*, 3:1366 §3526. •Muslim in *al-Ṣaḥīḥ*, 3:1315 §1688.

8

THE MOST GENEROUS

The Prophet ﷺ never said 'no' to anyone who asked him for something.[1] This was because he ﷺ was the most generous of people who would give to others even if he did not have any material wealth in his possession. The Companions ﵁ noted that he ﷺ would give others so much as though he did not fear poverty.[2] On one occasion, someone asked the Prophet Muhammad ﷺ to give him a flock of sheep in between two mountains, and the Prophet ﷺ accepted his request. When this person returned to his people, he said: "O my people! By God, accept Islam for Muhammad gives so generously as though he does not fear poverty."[3]

Even if the Prophet ﷺ did not have anything in his possession he would not turn away a beggar.[4] On one occasion, a man came to him asking for money, but the Prophet ﷺ did not have any. So, he ﷺ told the man to borrow money in his name, and when the time came he would pay off the debt.[5] Such was the generosity of this noble and blessed man!

---

[1] Set forth by •al-Bukhārī in *al-Ṣaḥīḥ*, 5:2244 §5686.

[2] Set forth by •Muslim in *al-Ṣaḥīḥ*, 4:1806 §2312.

[3] Ibid.

[4] Set forth by •Aḥmad b. Ḥanbal in *al-Musnad*, 2:33 §4880.

[5] Set forth by •al-Tirmidhī in *al-Shamāʾil al-Muḥammadiyya*, p. 294 §356. •al-Maqdisī in *al-Aḥādīth al-Mukhtāra*, 1:181 §88.

9

The Extraordinary Gentle

The Prophet Muhammad ﷺ taught gentleness, saying: "Shall I not inform you of whom the Fire is forbidden and who is forbidden for the Fire? He is the one who is near to people due to his good moral character, he is gentle in his temperament and he is considered very easy (to deal with) from his conduct (for such person, the Hellfire is forbidden)."[1]

God praises the Prophet ﷺ for his gentleness saying: ﴾*(O My Esteemed Beloved!) What a mercy of God that you are lenient with them! Had you been stern and hard-hearted, people would have deserted, scattering away from around you. So pardon them, and pray for their forgiveness, and consult them in (important) matters.*﴿ [Q.3:159.]

[1] Set forth by •Aḥmad b. Ḥanbal in *al-Musnad*, 1:415 §3938. •al-Tirmidhī in *al-Sunan*, 4:654 §2488.

10

The Possessor of a Soft Personality

The Prophet's personality was soft. He ﷺ disliked harshness and coarseness in behaviour. He ﷺ taught his followers to adopt softness in their behaviour and conduct as God loves gentleness over harshness. He ﷺ declared gentleness the chief of wisdom and encouraged his followers to show gentleness through acts of kindness as a means of protecting themselves from the Hellfire.[1]

From his own example, the beloved Prophet of God ﷺ showed kindness to others. On one occasion, when he ﷺ offered the prayer with his Companions ﷺ, he wanted to lengthen the prayer but did not do so because he could hear a child crying for his mother. The Prophet ﷺ knew the mother of the child would be in discomfort hearing her child cry, so out of his softness and kindness towards them, he ﷺ would shorten the prayer and end it as soon as possible.[2]

---

[1] Set forth by •Aḥmad b. Ḥanbal in *al-Musnad*, 1:415 §3938. •al-Tirmidhī in *al-Sunan*, 4:654 §2488.

[2] Set forth by •al-Bukhārī in *al-Ṣaḥīḥ*, 1:250 §677. •Muslim in *al-Ṣaḥīḥ*, 1:343 §470.

11

The Most Dignified in Speech

The Prophet ﷺ was known for his truthfulness and integrity. When we look at his personal conduct, we see that he was the most dignified in speech and that he spoke only to seek the pleasure of God.[1] The Prophet ﷺ was measured in his speech,[2] and he would not speak fast but at a balance and moderate pace such that if one were to count his words, they could be counted.[3] Anyone who listened to him ﷺ could understand him, and he would even speak to others in their own dialects.[4]

The Prophet ﷺ would remain silent most of the time and would not talk excessively.[5] His words were concise but full of meaning,[6] and he would never raise his voice when speaking, but he would smile and make others feel at ease.[7] He ﷺ would never cut anyone off whilst they are speaking unless he would

---

[1] Set forth by •al-Tirmidhī in *al-Shamāʾil al-Muḥammadiyya*, p. 291 §352. •al-Ṭabarānī in *al-Muʿjam al-Kabīr*, 22:158 §414.

[2] Set forth by •Abū Dāwūd in *al-Sunan*, 4:260 §4838.

[3] Set forth by •al-Bukhārī in *al-Ṣaḥīḥ*, 3:1307 §3374. •Muslim in *al-Ṣaḥīḥ*, 4:2298 §2493.

[4] Set forth by •Abū Dāwūd in *al-Sunan*, 4:261 §4839.

[5] Set forth by •al-Tirmidhī in *al-Shamāʾil al-Muḥammadiyya*, p. 184 §226. •al-Ṭabarānī in *al-Muʿjam al-Kabīr*, 22:156 §414.

[6] Set forth by •al-Tirmidhī in *al-Shamāʾil al-Muḥammadiyya*, p. 185 §226. •al-Ṭabarānī in *al-Muʿjam al-Kabīr*, 22:156 §414.

[7] Set forth by •Abū al-Shaykh al-Aṣbahānī in *Akhlāq al-Nabī* ﷺ, 2:17 §207. •al-Tirmidhī in *al-Shamāʾil al-Muḥammadiyya*, p. 291 §352.

forbid them from something wrong.[1] If he heard someone say something weird or strange, he would tell them to relate only what they saw or heard.[2]

[1] Set forth by •al-Tirmidhī in *al-Shamā'il al-Muḥammadiyya*, p. 291 §352. •al-Ṭabarānī in *al-Mu'jam al-Kabīr*, 22:158 §414.

[2] Set forth by •al-Tirmidhī in *al-Shamā'il al-Muḥammadiyya*, p. 291 §352. •al-Ṭabarānī in *al-Mu'jam al-Kabīr*, 22:156 §414.

12

The Paragon of Mercy

"Indeed, I am a mercy gifted (to the worlds),"[1] the Prophet Muhammad ﷺ said. Mercy is the defining character of the esteemed Prophet ﷺ; he ﷺ is mercy incarnate. God sent Prophet Muhammad ﷺ for no other purpose but to bring God's mercy to all creatures.[2] God say, ﴾*And, (O Esteemed Messenger,) We have not sent you but as a mercy for all the worlds.*﴿ [Q.21:107.] Thus, the mercy of Prophet Muhammad ﷺ is a universal blessing which encompasses all human beings, irrespective of their religion, race and gender.

---

[1] Set forth by •al-Dārimī in *al-Sunan*, 1:21 §15. •Ibn Abī Shayba in *al-Muṣannaf*, 6:325 §31782.

[2] Set forth by •Abū Dāwūd in *al-Sunan*, 4:215 §4659.

13

The Ambassador of Peace

The Prophet's political career is a testimony to his struggle to establish peace. Within a short period of ten years, he ﷺ united the warring Arab tribes under a single banner. This political feat had not been achieved in Arabia before this. The disunited Arab tribes, which once lived in a state of anarchy, were united under the rule of the law which subsequently brought peace to Arabia and the wider Middle East. The Prophet ﷺ achieved this by teaching the value of peace and security, such as his saying: "A Muslim is the one who provides peace to other Muslims through his words and deeds,"[1] and "The true believer is he whom people trust with regard to their lives and their properties."[2]

[1] Set forth by •al-Bukhārī in *al-Ṣaḥīḥ,* 1:13 §10.

[2] Set forth by •al-Tirmidhī in *al-Sunan*, 5:17 §2627

14

The Helper of the Weak and Indigent

Arabia, in the seventh century, was a tribal society where the rich and powerful devoured the weak. There was no recourse for the weak and indigent to redress the wrong done to them by the elites. However, the Prophet Muhammad ﷺ educated the Arabs to change their behaviour in their treatment of the weaker members of society. He said: “Shall I not inform you of the inhabitants of Paradise? Every humble person who is considered weak that if he were to swear an oath by God, God would fulfil it on his behalf. And shall I not inform you of the denizens of the Hellfire? They include every callous, quarrelsome and self-conceited person.’[1]

The esteemed Prophet ﷺ changed the perception of people in how they viewed the poor and needy in society. He ﷺ said: “God only gives aid to this community of Muslims by virtue of its weak ones.”[2] The Prophet ﷺ stood by the poor and indigent and spoke of their lofty status in the sight of God saying, “Look for me among your weak ones, for it is only by their virtue that you are granted provision and support.”[3] He

---

[1] Set forth by •al-Bukhārī in *al-Ṣaḥīḥ*, 5:2255 §5723. •Muslim in *al-Ṣaḥīḥ*, 4:2190 §2853.

[2] Set forth by •al-Bukhārī in *al-Ṣaḥīḥ*, 6:1061 §2739. •al-Nasāʾī in *al-Sunan*, 6:45 §3179; & in *al-Sunan al-Kubrā*, 3:345 §6181.

[3] Set forth by •Abū Dāwūd in *al-Sunan*, 3:32 §2594. •al-Tirmidhī in *al-Sunan*, 4:206 §1702.

encouraged his followers to honour them and to treat them with dignity, saying: "Love the poor and sit with them."[1]

[1] Set forth by •al-Ḥākim in *al-Mustadrak*, 4:368 §7947. •al-Mundhirī in *al-Targhīb wa al-Tarhīb*, 4:67 §4827.

15

The Carer for the Sick

Whenever God's Messenger ﷺ would visit a sick person, or whenever a sick person was brought to him, he would say, "Remove the affliction, O Lord of humankind. Heal [him or her], O Healer! There is no healing save Your healing—a healing that is not followed by sickness."[1]

He ﷺ brought hope to the sick person saying: 'If a believing person persistently does a righteous act but cannot accomplish it due to an illness or travel, it will be written for him as he did it when he was healthy and not in travel.'[2]

He ﷺ also encouraged the Muslims to visit and care for someone when they are sick. He ﷺ said: "Whoever visits his ailing Muslim brother, he will be walking in the garden of Paradise until he sits down, and when he sits down, mercy shall envelop him. If his visit is in the morning time, seventy thousand angels will send prayers on him, until he enters the evening time. And if his visit is in the evening, seventy thousand angels will send prayers on him, until he enters the morning time."[3]

---

[1] Set forth by •al-Bukhārī in *al-Ṣaḥīḥ*, 5:2147 §5351. •Muslim in *al-Ṣaḥīḥ*, 4:1722 §2191.

[2] Set forth by •Abū Dāwūd in *al-Sunan*, 3:183 §3091.

[3] Set forth by •Abū Dāwūd in *al-Sunan*, 3:185 §3098. •Ibn Mājah in *al-Sunan*, 1:463 §1442.

16

The Emancipator of Slaves

Prophet Muhammad ﷺ laid the foundation for the elimination of slavery in the pre-modern world. Through his Prophetic wisdom, he instituted a gradual and systematic method of bringing an end to slavery. He tied religious observance and piety with the freeing of slaves, and he had outlawed unjust economic practices that bound people into slavery. The Prophet ﷺ said: "Whoever frees a believing slave, then for every part that he freed, God shall free a part of him from the Hellfire."[1]

The Prophet Muhammad ﷺ also instituted rights for slaves. He ﷺ said: "Your slaves are your brothers whom God has placed under your authority, so whoever has a brother under his authority, should feed him from what he eats and clothe him with what he wears. Do not burden them with what is too much for them to bear. When you ask them of (a difficult task), assist them."[2]

[1] Set forth by •al-Bukhārī in *al-Ṣaḥīḥ*, 2:891 §2381. •Muslim in *al-Ṣaḥīḥ*, 2:1147 §1509.

[2] Set forth by •al-Bukhārī in *al-Ṣaḥīḥ*, 1:20 §30. •Muslim in *al-Ṣaḥīḥ*, 3:1283 §1661.

17

The Protector of Refugees

The teachings of Prophet Muhammad ﷺ granted protection to refugees. Addressing issues of social justice the Qurʾān specifically says: ﴾*And if any of the idolaters seeks asylum with you, provide him with protection until he listens to the Words of Allah. Then escort him to his haven. This is because these people do not possess the knowledge (of the truth).*﴿ [Q.9:6.]

He ﷺ spoke constantly and consistently to his Companions ﷺ about the benefits and the necessity of helping those in need. He said: "Whoever grants respite to someone in difficulty or alleviates him, God will shade him on the Day of Resurrection when there is no shade but His."[1]

[1] Set forth by •Aḥmad b. Ḥanbal in *al-Musnad*, 2:359 §8696. •al-Tirmidhī in *al-Sunan*, 3:599 §1306.

18

The Advocate for Animal Rights

From the mercy of Prophet Muhammad ﷺ is his mercy towards animals. He taught his followers that even animals have rights and that we must show them mercy and kindness. He warned his Companions from harming or abusing their animals. On one occasion, the Prophet ﷺ came across an emaciated camel that was tied up to a column. Seeing this distressed him. He ﷺ told his Companions to fear God with respect to these animals,[1] as they will be held accountable on the Day of Judgement in their treatment regarding them.

On another occasion, God's Messenger ﷺ passed by a man who was milking a sheep. He ﷺ said: "When you milk her, leave some for her lamb because it is one of the gentlest of animals."[2]

Speaking of the rights of animals, he ﷺ also said: "Ride these animals as long as they are healthy, and do not take them as seats (when not riding)."[3] And: 'God orders you to treat these beasts of burden well when you put them to work and keep them at their places, and when afflicted with drought, hasten with them until they are agile and energetic.'"[4]

---

[1] Set forth by •Aḥmad b. Ḥanbal in *al-Musnad*, 1:205 §1754. •Abū Dāwūd in *al-Sunan*, 3:23 §2549.

[2] Set forth by •al-Ṭabarānī *al-Muʿjam al-Awsaṭ*, 1:271 §885.

[3] Set forth by •Aḥmad b. Ḥanbal in *al-Musnad*, 3:440 §15677. •al-Dārimī in *al-Sunan*, 2:371 §2668.

[4] Set forth by •Ḥārith in *al-Musnad*, 2:838 §885.

19

The First to Speak Against Racism

On one occasion, a Companion of the Prophet ﷺ disparagingly said to Bilāl, "You son of a black woman." Hearing this, the Prophet ﷺ swiftly rebuked this Companion for his racism saying, "Are you taunting him about his mother? There is still some influence of ignorance in you."[1]

The Prophet Muhammad ﷺ unequivocally condemned racism when he said: "All mankind is descended from Adam and Eve. An Arab has no superiority over a non-Arab. And a non-Arab has no superiority over an Arab. A white person has no superiority over a black person, nor a black person has any superiority over a white person, except by piety and good action."[2] This declaration was the first of its kind in human history.

---

[1] Set forth by •al-Bukhārī in *al-Ṣaḥīḥ*, 1:20 §30.

[2] Set forth by •Aḥmad b. Ḥanbal in *al-Musnad*, 5:411 §23536. •Abū Nuʿaym in *Ḥilya al-Awliyāʾ*, 3:100.

20

The Honourer of People's Humanity

Once a funeral procession passed by and the Prophet ﷺ stood up for it out of respect. The Companions ﷺ stood up with him. They then asked, 'O Messenger of God! That was the funeral of a Jew [so why did you stand]?' The Prophet of God ﷺ replied, "When you see a funeral procession, you should stand up."[1]

From this exemplary conduct, we see that the Holy Prophet ﷺ honoured the humanity of people by standing up for their funeral. It did not matter whether the person is a Muslim or not, a person's dignity matters because all people, irrespective of their beliefs, are sacred and are thus worthy of honour and respect on account of their humanity. In another narration, it is reported that he ﷺ said, "Isn't he a soul created by God?"[2]

---

[1] Set forth by •al-Bukhārī in *al-Ṣaḥīḥ*, 1:441 §1249. •Muslim in *al-Ṣaḥīḥ*, 2:660 §960.

[2] Set forth by •al-Bukhārī in *al-Ṣaḥīḥ*, 1:441 §1250. •Muslim in *al-Ṣaḥīḥ*, 2:661 §961.

21

The Facilitator of Ease for People

Prophet Muhammad ﷺ once declared: "Indeed, God did not send me to be harsh or cause harm; He sent me to teach and make things easy!"[1] It is related by the Companions ﷺ that the Prophet ﷺ used to lighten people's burden and remove difficulties from them. If he was given two options that were good, he would always choose the easier of the two options.[2] This facilitation was to make life easier for people and to avoid undue hardships and difficulties.

[1] Set forth by •Muslim in *al-Ṣaḥīḥ*, 2:1104 §1478.

[2] Set forth by •al-Bukhārī in *al-Ṣaḥīḥ*, 3:1306 §3367. •Muslim in *al-Ṣaḥīḥ*, 4:1813 §2327.

22

The Kindest to His Family

Prophet Muhammad ﷺ gave great importance to maintain family ties and serving one's family. He always fulfilled his obligations to his family and relatives and warned against cutting the ties of kinship. He declared doing so among the major sins. He constantly encouraged his followers to take care of their relatives and to be good towards their family and dependants. The Prophet ﷺ led by example and would help his family in the household chores and show them much attention and love. He ﷺ set the standard to measure true excellence by saying: "The best of you is he who is best toward his family, and I am the best of you toward my family."[1]

[1] Set forth by •al-Tirmidhī in *al-Sunan*, 5:709 §3895. •Ibn Mājah in *al-Sunan*, 1:636 §1977.

23

The Caretaker of Widows and Orphans

The Prophet ﷺ used to look after the widows and orphans and he taught his followers to look after them too. He ﷺ said: "The one who strives in caring for a widow or a poor person is like the one who strives in the path of God."[1] In another narration, he ﷺ said: "I and the caretaker of an orphan shall be in Paradise like this," and he pointed with his index and middle finger and separated them a bit.[2]

He highlighted the plights of orphans and taught his followers their rights. He ﷺ said: "The best house among the Muslims is the house in which resides an orphan who is treated well. And the worst house among the Muslims is the house in which resides an orphan who is treated badly."[3] On another occasion, he said: "A man once complained about his hard heart to God's Messenger, and so the Prophet ﷺ told him, "If you wish for your heart to become soft, feed the poor and take care of the orphan."[4]

---

[1] Set forth by •al-Bukhārī in *al-Ṣaḥīḥ*, 5:2047 §5038. •Muslim in *al-Ṣaḥiḥ*, 4:2286 §2982.

[2] Set forth by •al-Bukhārī in *al-Ṣaḥīḥ*, 5:2032 §4998. •Abū Dāwūd in *al-Sunan*, 4:338 §5150.

[3] Set forth by •Ibn Mājah in *al-Sunan*, 2:1213 §3679. •al-Bukhārī in *al-Adab al-Mufrad*, p. 61 §137.

[4] Set forth by •Aḥmad b. Ḥanbal in *al-Musnad*, 2:263 §7566. •ʿAbd b. Ḥumayd in *al-Musnad*, 1:417 §1426.

24

An Advocate for Women's Rights and Dignity

"The most perfect of the believers, where faith is concerned, is the finest of them in moral character, and the best of you are the ones who treat their women best,"[1] the Prophet Muhammad ﷺ declared. In Arabia, women were treated like property and were stripped off their rights. They could be inherited and were not given any status in society. The Prophet ﷺ changed the way the Arabs viewed women. He advocated the rights of women and upheld their dignity. He declared them partners to men and declared their immunity in warfare. Women were legislated a right to initiate divorce, receive inheritance and own property. They had a right to education and even partake in the running of state affairs. The Prophet ﷺ honoured women by acknowledging the critical role played in upbringing their children by declaring the right of a mother three times more than the right of the father.[2] He promised Paradise to any man who took care of his daughters[3] at a time when the Arabs deemed daughters to be a blemish to their family honour and found no qualm in burying them alive. In doing so, he ﷺ

---

[1] Set forth by •al-Bukhārī in *al-Ṣaḥīḥ*, 3:1006 §2591, 2593. •Muslim in *al-Ṣaḥīḥ*, 3:1250 §1628.

[2] Set forth by •al-Bukhārī in *al-Ṣaḥīḥ*, 5:2227 §5262. •Muslim in *al-Ṣaḥīḥ*, 4:1974 §2548.

[3] Set forth by •Aḥmad b. Ḥanbal in *al-Musnad*, 3:97 §11943. •Abū Dāwūd in *al-Sunan*, 4:338 §5147.

changed the perception of society and enshrined honouring of women as a part and parcel of piety and religiosity.

25

The Affectionate to Children

Being mercy incarnate, the esteemed emissary of God ﷺ showed great love and affection towards children. He never scolded any child nor showed them contempt. The young Anas b. Mālik ؓ recounting his experience said: "I served the Prophet ﷺ for 10 years. He never once said 'fie' to me [i.e. used an expression to show disapproval]. If I did something that I shouldn't have done, he did not say to me 'why did you do it?', and if I left out something that I should've done, he did not say 'why didn't you do it'[1]... the Prophet ﷺ never once rebuked me for doing something wrong, even if others rebuked me. He would prevent others from rebuking me, saying: "Leave him."[2]

On another occasion, a group of Bedouins went to see God's Messenger ﷺ. They asked, 'Do you kiss your children?' They [the Companions ؓ] said, 'Yes.' The Bedouins said, 'By God! As for us, we do not kiss [our children].' Upon (hearing) this, God's Messenger ﷺ said, 'What can I do if God has removed mercy from your hearts?'"[3] Showing love and affection towards children is an act of mercy and the Companions ؓ stated that

---

[1] Set forth by •al-Bukhārī in *al-Ṣaḥīḥ*, 5:2245 §5691. •Muslim in *al-Ṣaḥīḥ*, 4:1804 §2309.

[2] Set forth by •Aḥmad b. Ḥanbal in *al-Musnad*, 3:231 §13442. •Ibn Abī ʿĀṣim in *al-Sunna*, 1:157 §355.

[3] Set forth by •al-Bukhārī in *al-Ṣaḥīḥ*, 5:2235 §5652. •Muslim in *al-Ṣaḥīḥ*, 4:1808 §2317.

they have never seen anyone more merciful towards children than the Prophet Muhammad ﷺ.[1]

[1] Set forth by •Ibn ʿAsākir in *Tārīkh Madīna Dimashq*, 4:88.

26

The Best Neighbour

The Prophet Muhammad ﷺ did not just teach his followers to be good to their friends and family, but he also taught the rights of neighbours. On one occasion, he said, "By God, he is not a believer; by God, he is not a believer; by God, he is not a believer, one whose neighbours are not secure from his harm."[1]

The Prophet ﷺ did not discriminate between any of his neighbours, even if they were not Muslims and they did not believe in him. He ﷺ looked after his neighbours and he enjoined the Muslims to look after their neighbours saying, "He is not a believer who spends the night satiated to his full whilst knowing that his neighbour goes to sleep hungry."[2]

[1] Set forth by •al-Bukhārī in *al-Ṣaḥīḥ*, 5:2240 §5670. •Muslim in *al-Ṣaḥīḥ*, 1:68 §46.

[2] Set forth by •al-Bukhārī in *al-Adab al-Mufrad*, p. 52 §112. •al-Ṭabarānī in *al-Muʿjam al-Kabīr*, 12:154 §12741.

27

The Appreciative of People's Efforts

The Prophet Muhammad ﷺ was appreciative of people's efforts and their devotion. On one occasion he passed by a neighbourhood of Medina and came across a group of children who were playing the tambourine. They sang the words: "We are the young girls of Banū al-Najjār. What an excellent neighbour is Muhammad!" The Prophet ﷺ appreciating their efforts, replied, "Certainly, God knows that I love you too!"[1]

[1] Set forth by •Ibn Mājah in *al-Sunan*, 1:612 §1899. •Abū Yaʿlā in *al-Musnad*, 6:134 §3409.

28

The Most Respectful of Others

God instructed the Prophet Muhammad ﷺ to give the following command to the Muslims: "O believers! Let no community ridicule another community. It is likely that they may be better than those (who ridicule). Nor should women make fun of other women. It is likely that they may be better than those (who make fun). And do not offend or find fault with one another, nor call each other names. Calling someone wicked or indecent after (he embraces) faith is an extremely evil name. And those who do not turn to God in repentance, it is they who are the wrongdoers."[1]

[1] Qur'ān 49:11.

29

The True Humanitarian and Philanthropist

The Prophet Muhammad ﷺ truly cared about others, bettering the lives of the weak and indigent. To achieve this lofty goal, he taught his followers the true meaning of charity. He ﷺ said: "It is a duty upon every Muslim to give charity." The Companions ﷺ asked him, "O Prophet of God! What about the one who does not find anything [to spend in charity]?" He ﷺ replied, "Let him work with his hands, benefitting himself, and let him then spend in charity." The Companions ﷺ asked, "And what if he cannot find [work]?" He ﷺ replied, "Then let him assist someone wronged and needy." The Companions ﷺ asked, "And what if he cannot find (anyone in need)?" He replied, "Then let him do good and abstain from evil, for that will be his charity."[1] It is also reported that he – peace and blessings upon him – said: "Smiling at your brother is charity."[2]

[1] Set forth by •al-Bukhārī in *al-Ṣaḥīḥ*, 2:524 §1376. •Muslim in *al-Ṣaḥīḥ*, 2:699 §1008.

[2] Set forth by •al-Tirmidhī in *al-Sunan*, 4:339 §1956. •Ibn Ḥibbān in *al-Ṣaḥīḥ*, 2:286 §529.

30

The Ambassador of Interfaith Harmony

God gave the following commandment to Prophet Muhammad ﷺ: ﴾*Say: 'O People of the Book (i.e. Christians and Jews), come to that matter which is common between us and you (namely that): we shall worship none other than God, and we shall not associate any partner with Him. Nor shall anyone of us take one another as Lords apart from God. Then if they turn away, say: Bear witness that we are but God's obedient servants.*﴿ [Q.64:3.]

In his lifetime, Prophet Muhammad ﷺ permitted a Christian delegation from Najrān to pray in his mosque when they visited Medina. This delegation came to debate him and challenge his message, but in spite of this, he permitted them to pray in his mosque, thus showing the importance of fostering dialogue and co-operation between the adherents of different religions.[1]

[1] Set forth by •al-Bayhaqī in *Dalā'il al-Nubuwwa*, 5:382. •Ibn Saʿd in *al-Ṭabaqāt al-Kubrā*, 1:357. •Ibn Hishām in *al-Sīra al-Nabawiyya*, 2:239–240.

31

The Striver for Social Cohesion

The Prophet Muhammad ﷺ strove for social cohesion. ʿAbd Allāh b. Salām, who was a Jewish Rabbi, recounts the anecdote of the first time he saw the Prophet ﷺ. Recounting this moment, he said: "When the Messenger of God – peace and blessings be upon him – came to Medina, the people rushed towards him and it was said, "The Messenger of God has come!" I came along with the people to see him, and when I looked at the face of the Messenger of God, I realised that his face was not the face of a liar. The first thing he said was: "O people, spread peace, feed the hungry, and pray at night when people are sleeping, you will enter Paradise in peace."[1]

[1] Set forth by •al-Tirmidhī in *al-Sunan*, 4:652 §2485. •Ibn Mājah in *al-Sunan*, 1:423 §1334.

32

The Honourer of People of Different Ethnicities

Every human being has an inviolable sanctity as they are created uniquely by God and endowed with life. Teaching this divine principle, the Prophet ﷺ upheld the honour of all people irrespective of their race or ethnicity. Once, during the Prophet's venerable life, there was a black woman who used to clean the Mosque. God's Messenger ﷺ did not see her for a few days, so he enquired about her. The Companions ؓ told him that she had died. The Prophet ﷺ visibly distressed by this news asked, "Why did you not inform me?" It was as if they deemed her unimportant. The Prophet ﷺ asked to be shown her grave so that he could pray for her. When he reached her grave, he prayed for her and told his Companions ؓ: "Indeed, these graves are filled with darkness for their inhabitants, but God fills them with light due to my prayers over them."[1] Through his excellent conduct, Prophet Muhammad ﷺ demonstrated the importance and worth of every human being and he did not discriminate against anyone because of their race, colour, or ethnicity.

---

[1] Set forth by •al-Bukhārī in *al-Ṣaḥīḥ*, 1:175–176, 448 §§446, 2172. •Muslim in *al-Ṣaḥīḥ*, 2:659 §956.

33

The Remover of Enmity and Hatred

The Prophet ﷺ advocated for social integration and maintaining ties with people. When the Prophet ﷺ emigrated to Medina, he created a city-state which united peoples of different tribes and religions. One of the first pacts he made was the pact of brotherhood between the Aws and Khazraj tribes, who were broiled in a bitter civil war over many generations. Through the message of Islam, the beloved Prophet of God ﷺ united the people of these two tribes and ended their renowned feud.

Another pact was the brotherhood between the Helpers of Medina and the Emigrants from Mecca. He took one person from the Helpers of Medina and made him a brother of one of the people among the Emigrants of Mecca. He taught the Helpers to share their resources with the Emigrants and to remove the disparity in wealth between them.[1] He also made a pact between the Muslims and Jews and united them as a single nation. All of these were the efforts the Prophet ﷺ made to bring people together and to remove hatred between them.

On one occasion the beloved Prophet ﷺ said: "The glory of the believers lies in brotherhood. They do not subject each other to torture, coercion, oppression, terrorism and vandalism. Nor do they usurp on another's wealth or are thirsty for each

[1] Set forth by •Ibn Saʿd in *al-Ṭabaqāt al-Kubrā*, 1:238. •al-Ṣāliḥī in *Subul al-Hudā wa al-Rishād*, 3:527. •Ibn Hishām in *al-Sīra al-Nabawiyya*, 2:529–533.

other's blood. They protect and love each other and hide each other's fault."[1]

[1] Set forth by •al-Bukhārī in *al-Ṣaḥīḥ*, 2:862 §2310. •Muslim in *al-Ṣaḥīḥ*, 4:1996 §2580.

34

The Opposer of Anti-Semitism

There used to be a Jewish boy who would serve the Prophet ﷺ. The Prophet ﷺ treated him with affection as he did with other children. On one occasion the boy fell ill, so the Prophet ﷺ went to visit him. He ﷺ sat near his head and said to him, 'Embrace Islam.' The boy then looked at his father who was with him, and his father said, 'Obey Abū al-Qāsim [the Prophet].' The boy embraced Islam (and then died). The Prophet ﷺ departed, saying, 'All praise is due to God, Who saved him from the Hellfire.'[1]

On another occasion, a Jewess brought poisoned meat of a sheep to God's Messenger ﷺ and he ate a little from it. After her plot was discovered, as the poison became manifest, she was brought to God's Messenger ﷺ and he asked her why she did it. She replied, 'I wanted to assassinate you.' God's Messenger ﷺ said, 'God will not empower you to do it.' The Companions ؓ submitted, 'Shall we not kill her?' He ﷺ replied, 'No.' Thus, he forgave the Jewess for the wrong she did to him ﷺ.[2]

---

[1] Set forth by •al-Bukhārī in *al-Ṣaḥīḥ*, 1:455 §1290. •Abū Dāwūd in *al-Sunan*, 3:185 §3095.

[2] Set forth by •al-Bukhārī in *al-Ṣaḥīḥ*, 2:923 §2474. •Muslim in *al-Ṣaḥīḥ*, 4:1721 §2190.

35

The Acknowledger of Virtues

When the pagan Meccan's hostility against the Muslims became unbearably brutal, the Prophet ﷺ commanded a group of them to migrate to Abyssinia, even though Abyssinia was a Christian country and its ruler, the Negus, was a Christian. Since the repute of the King Negus reached the Prophet ﷺ as a just and kind ruler, he selected the Christian country for the first and second migration. It was declared as an "Abode of Peace" for the Muslims.[1]

Muṭᶜim b. ᶜAdī was an idolater. Concerning him, the Prophet Muhammad ﷺ said: "Were Muṭᶜim b. ᶜAdī alive and interceded with me for these sinful people, I would definitely forgive them for his sake."[2] And concerning, Mukhayriq, a Jewish Rabbi, he said: "Mukhayriq is the best of the Jews."[3]

---

[1] Set forth by •Ibn Hishām in *al-Sīra al-Nabawiyya*, 2:176–177. •al-Ṭabarī in *Tārīkh al-Umam wa al-Mulūk*, 1:547.

[2] Set forth by •al-Bukhārī in *al-Ṣaḥīḥ*, 3:1143 §2970. •ᶜAbd al-Razzāq in *al-Muṣannaf*, 5:209 §9400.

[3] Set forth by •Ibn Hishām in *al-Sīra al-Nabawiyya*, 3:51. •Ibn ᶜAsākir in *Tārīkh Madīna Dimashq*, 10:229. •Ibn Saᶜd in *al-Ṭabaqāt al-Kubrā*, 1:501.

36

The Proponent of Love

Prophet Muhammad ﷺ taught that the seed of faith is love. This seed of faith is the love of God, His Prophet ﷺ, love for the people of God and love of all good actions that are loved by Him. He said that no person can be a true believer until he loves him ﷺ more than anyone in creation.[1] True faith is rooted in love and without it, it cannot grow into a fruitful tree that gives good to everyone around it.

The Prophet ﷺ himself is characterised by his love for God and the believers. Concerning his love for the believers, God says in the Qurʾān: ﴾*Surely, a (Glorious) Messenger from amongst yourselves has come to you. Your suffering and distress (becomes) grievously heavy on him. (O humankind,) he is ardently desirous of your (betterment and guidance. And) he is most (deeply) clement and merciful to the believers.*﴿ [Q.9:128.]

[1] Set forth by •al-Bukhārī in *al-Ṣaḥīḥ*, 1:14 §15. •Muslim in *al-Ṣaḥīḥ*, 1:67 §44.

37

The Respectful of Other Faiths

Being a mercy to all of humanity, the Prophet Muhammad ﷺ treated all people with fairness and kindness. It did not matter what religion one belonged to, the Prophet ﷺ fulfilled his oaths and made true his promises. He ﷺ did not discriminate between any people. On one occasion, the Prophet ﷺ passed by a meeting which was attended by Muslims, polytheists and Jews and he greeted them all equally with the salutation of peace.[1]

[1] Set forth by •ʿAbd al-Razzāq in *al-Muṣannaf*, 6:12 §9844 & 10:392 §19463. •Abū ʿUwāna in *al-Musnad*, 4:345 §6915. •al-Bayhaqī in *al-Sunan al-Kubrā*, 4:18 §6619.

38

The Protector of Non-Muslims

"Whoever kills a non-Muslim under a treaty unjustly, God shall forbid him Paradise," the Prophet ﷺ declared.[1] The beloved Messenger of God ﷺ did not just protect non-Muslims and declare their lives inviolable, he actively protected them by warning his followers not to harm non-Muslims who are living amongst them. In unequivocal words, he said: "Anyone who kills a non-Muslim under the treaty will not smell the fragrance of Paradise, even though its fragrance can be smelled at a distance of forty years."[2] This was a stern warning for the Muslims to protect the lives of non-Muslims and not to violate their sanctity as all life is sacred.

---

[1] Set forth by •al-Nasāʾī in *al-Sunan*, 8:24 §4747. •Aḥmad b. Ḥanbal in *al-Sunan*, 5:36, 38 §20393, 20419. •Abū Dāwūd in *al-Sunan*, 3:83 §2760.

[2] Set forth by •al-Bukhārī in *al-Ṣaḥīḥ*, 3:1155 §2995. •Ibn Mājah in *al-Sunan*, 2:896 §2686.

39

The Reverent of the Past Prophets

Prophet Muhammad ﷺ was the descendant of Prophet Abraham. It was said that he resembled his grandfather Prophet Abraham in appearance. Through the Qurʾān, he ﷺ taught his followers to respect all the past Prophets, such as Prophets Adam, Noah, Abraham, Moses and Jesus, and made belief in their Prophethood an essential tenant of faith without which a person cannot be declared a Muslim. He ﷺ taught his followers not to create any disparity between him and the other Prophets as they were all sent by God.[1]

[1] Set forth by •al-Bukhārī in *al-Ṣaḥīḥ*, 6:2534 §6518. •Muslim in *al-Ṣaḥīḥ*, 4:1845 §2374.

40

The Greatest Forgiver

"I have been commanded with forgiveness, therefore do not fight," the Prophet Muhammad ﷺ said. The Prophet ﷺ faced many great hardships and difficulties during his 23-year Prophetic mission, but he forgave his transgressors. One such example was on the occasion of his preaching in Ṭāʾif. The chiefs of the town set the children and slaves loose to hurl pebbles at the Prophet ﷺ which resulted in his blessed body being soaked in blood. So much blood had been shed that the blessed soles of his feet were stuck to his sandals. Seeing this, the nearby angels in charge of the mountains asked the Prophet ﷺ to punish the people of Ṭāʾif by crushing them in between the mountains but the Prophet ﷺ did not permit the angels to do so and instead forgave the people and prayed for their children that they would be gifted the blessing of faith.[1] And so, within the Prophet's lifetime, the people of Ṭāʾif accepted Islam willingly and the Prophet ﷺ set forgiveness and mercy as his noble example and precedent.

[1] Set forth by •al-Bukhārī in *al-Ṣaḥīḥ*, 3:1180 §3059. •Muslim in *al-Ṣaḥīḥ*, 3:1420 §1795.

41

The Rejecter of Revenge

The Prophet Muhammad ﷺ spent 13 years preaching in Mecca. During this time, the people of Mecca had directed all kinds of abuse against the Prophet ﷺ, his Family ﷺ and Companions ﷺ. After 13 years of peaceful preaching, he was forced to leave his homeland to emigrate to the small oasis of Yathrib over 250 miles away. Even after having emigrated, the Meccans pursued the Prophet ﷺ and sent armies to invade his place of emigration and to decimate the religion of Islam. However, 10 years later, the Prophet ﷺ returned to Mecca with an army of 10,000 soldiers to conquer Mecca. On this day of the conquest, one of the Companions ﷺ called out to the people of Mecca and said: "Today is the day of revenge!" When the Prophet Muhammad ﷺ was informed of this statement, he ﷺ rejected it and said, "Today is the Day of Forgiveness."[1]

[1] Set forth by •Ibn ʿAsākir in *Tārīkh Madīna Dimashq*, 23:454. •Ibn ʿAbd al-Barr in *al-Istīʿāb*, 2:597. •al-Ḥalabī in *al-Sīra al-Ḥalabiyya*, 3:22.

42

The Most Lenient in Dealings

One of the striking qualities of Prophet Muhammad ﷺ is his leniency in his treatment of others. God praises Prophet Muhammad ﷺ in the Qur'ān by emphasising his leniency and declaring it His favour. God says: ﴾*(O My Esteemed Beloved!) What a mercy of God that you are lenient with them! Had you been stern and hard-hearted, people would have deserted, scattering away from around you. So, pardon them, and pray for their forgiveness, and consult them in (important) matters.*﴿ [Q.3:159.]

Such was the Prophet's leniency that once a Bedouin (Desert Arab) urinated in the mosque. The Prophet's Companions ﷺ were incensed by this disrespectful act and were about to rough him up. But the Prophet Muhammad ﷺ stopped them and calmed the situation down by commanding his Companions ﷺ to clean the place by placing a bucket of water over the urine. He then counselled his Companions ﷺ by teaching them the principle of leniency saying: "You have been sent to facilitate ease and not to cause difficulty and hardship."[1]

[1] Set forth by •al-Bukhārī in *al-Ṣaḥīḥ*, 1:89 §217. •Aḥmad b. Ḥanbal in *al-Musnad*, 2:282 §7786.

43

THE MOST FORBEARING AND PATIENT

A Companion once narrated an incident highlighting the forbearing and patient nature of Prophet Muhammad ﷺ. He said: "I was walking with the Prophet ﷺ and he was wearing a mantle with a thick border. We met a Bedouin on the way. The Bedouin pulled the mantle so violently that I noticed the side of the Prophet's shoulder affected by the friction of the mantle's border because of the violent pull. The Bedouin said, "Give me some of God's wealth that is with you." God's Messenger ﷺ turned and looked at him smiling and ordered that some wealth be given to him."[1]

Such was the great level of forbearance of the Prophet Muhammad ﷺ. Let alone patience with the harm caused by the Bedouin, the beloved Prophet of God ﷺ also showed him kindness by giving him the money that he asked for. This is certainly an extraordinary level of mercy that is not common to see.

[1] Set forth by •al-Bukhārī in *al-Ṣaḥīḥ*, 3:1148 §2980. •Muslim in *al-Ṣaḥīḥ*, 2:730 §1057. •Aḥmad b. Ḥanbal in *al-Musnad*, 3:153 §12570.

44

The Controller of Anger

The beloved Prophet Muhammad ﷺ was the most patient and forbearing of people.[1] He ﷺ would always control his anger and never let his anger get hold of him. He ﷺ would never get angry over worldly matters but he would show his anger only for just causes and for the sake of defending victims.[2] He ﷺ taught his followers to control their anger and not to get angry except for the sake of God, such as fighting against oppression and injustice.

If something annoyed the Prophet ﷺ he would walk away from it and avoid it.[3] He ﷺ would never get angry for personal reasons, and he was never vindictive or sought revenge. On one occasion, a Bedouin asked the Prophet ﷺ for assistance, and after assisting him with his need, the Prophet ﷺ asked, "Have I been good to you?" The Bedouin out of his ingratitude replied 'No.' This angered the Muslims and they got up to deal with him, but the Prophet ﷺ gently replied to them to leave him alone and not to say anything to him.[4]

1 Set forth by •Abū al-Shaykh al-Aṣbahānī in *Akhlāq al-Nabī wa Ādābihi*, 1:468 §175.

2 Set forth by •al-Tirmidhī in *al-Shamā'il al-Muḥammadiyya*, p. 185 §226. •al-Ṭabarānī in *al-Mu'jam al-Kabīr*, 22:156 §414.

3 Ibid.

4 Set forth by •Abū al-Shaykh al-Aṣbahānī in *Akhlāq al-Nabī wa Ādābihi*, 1:472 §177. •al-Ghazālī in *Iḥyā' 'Ulūm al-Dīn*, 2:379. •al-Haythamī in *Majma' al-Zawā'id*, 9:16. •Ibn Kathīr in *Tafsīr al-Qur'ān al-'Aẓīm*, 2:405.

45

The One Who Does not Curse

The Prophetic character is defined by his good temperament and pleasant nature. He ﷺ would never use foul words or speak harshly.[1] He avoided all indecent and ungodly manners of speech. It was not from his practice to curse others. Once the Companions ﷺ wanted the Prophet ﷺ to invoke God's curse on the pagans, but the Prophet ﷺ gently replied: "I was not sent as one who curses, rather I was sent as a mercy."[2] Emulating the Prophetic character, many of the great sages and spiritual masters in Islamic history would avoid cursing people who fell into cycles of sin and addiction. Instead, they would pray for their rehabilitation and attempt to reform their behaviour through sincere counsel and acts of kindness and gentleness.

---

[1] Set forth by •al-Bukhārī in *al-Ṣaḥīḥ*, 3:1305 §3366. •Muslim in *al-Ṣaḥīḥ*, 4:1810 §2321.

[2] Set forth by •Muslim in *al-Ṣaḥīḥ*, 4:2006 §2599. •al-Bukhārī in *al-Adab al-Mufrad*, p. 119 §321. •Abū Yaʿlā in *al-Musnad*, 11:35 §6174.

46

The Most Merciful Towards the Sinners

The mercy of the Prophet ﷺ encompasses all people, even those who are sinners. This mercy will become most perceptible on the Day of Judgement when God will judge all of humanity for their actions and give people their just recompense for their actions. On that day, the justice of God will be dominant and there will be no chance of escape from His wrath and punishment. The whole of humanity will be in trouble that day and will look towards Prophet Muhammad ﷺ to be their intercessor to save them from the punishment. Many will be saved from the Hellfire through the intercession of the Prophet Muhammad ﷺ and many will be taken out of the Hellfire on account of it. The Prophet ﷺ will intercede for all the sinners until the last of them are freed from the fire of Hell.[1]

Concerning this intercession, the esteemed Prophet ﷺ said, "My intercession is for the sinners of my nation."[2] Giving details about this intercession, he ﷺ said, "I was given an option between intercession and half of my nation entering Paradise, and I chose the intercession because it is more encompassing. Do you think the intercession is for the pious and righteous? No, in fact it is for the sinners and the wrongdoers."[3]

---

[1] Set forth by •al-Bukhārī in *al-Ṣaḥīḥ*, 6:2695–2696 §6975. •Muslim in *al-Ṣaḥīḥ*, 1:180 §193.

[2] Set forth by •Aḥmad b. Ḥanbal in *al-Musnad*, 3:213 §13245. •al-Tirmidhī in *al-Sunan*, 4:625 §2436.

[3] Set forth by •Aḥmad b. Ḥanbal in *al-Musnad*, 2:75 §5452. •Ibn Abī ʿĀṣim in *al-Sunna*, 2:368 §791.

This illuminating explanation shows the mercy of the Prophet Muhammad ﷺ that by being 'God's Beloved' and a 'Mercy for all mankind', he ﷺ will redeem the sinners from the divine wrath and punishment. Through his intercession, he ﷺ extended this mercy to those who are in dire need without the need for a blood sacrifice. This reality demonstrates the purity of Islam's doctrine of salvation and the encompassing mercy of Prophet Muhammad ﷺ.

47

The Provider of the Most Beautiful Company

His Companions ﷺ used to recall what it was like being in his company. One of them said, "His gathering was a gathering of knowledge."[1] Another said, "He used to give every attendant his due recognition, and none would feel that anyone was more honoured than him."[2] A third said, "He would patiently attend to anyone who sat with him to discuss his need, and he would never take his leave until the person in need would get up first."[3]

The Prophet ﷺ was highly meticulous and respectable. He would never blow his nose or spit in front of others in his gatherings.[4] Voices would not be raised;[5] elders would be treated with honour and dignity and the young would be treated with love and kindness.[6] The Prophet ﷺ would not allow someone to be neglected or to be kept out of the gathering and

[1] Set forth by •al-Tirmidhī in *al-Shamā'il al-Muḥammadiyya*, p. 278 §337.

[2] Ibid.

[3] Set forth by •al-Tirmidhī in *al-Shamā'il al-Muḥammadiyya*, p. 278 §337. •al-Ṭabarānī in *al-Mu'jam al-Kabīr*, 22:158 §414.

[4] Set forth by •Abū Dāwūd in *al-Marāsīl*, p. 344 §505. •Qāḍī 'Iyāḍ in *al-Shifā'*, p. 181.

[5] Set forth by •al-Tirmidhī in *al-Shamā'il al-Muḥammadiyya*, p. 278 §337. •al-Ṭabarānī in *al-Mu'jam al-Kabīr*, 22:158 §414.

[6] Ibid.

he would not allow anyone's honour or dignity to be violated. His beautiful gatherings were marked by honour and respect.

48

The Most Loving towards His Followers

The pagans of Mecca would notice the love and devotion the Companions ﷺ would show to Prophet Muhammad ﷺ. Even with the passing of 14 centuries, the Muslims today show immense love and devotion to their Prophet ﷺ unlike any other community. This love and devotion is a reflection of the Prophet's own love and mercy for his followers, and even today, the Prophet ﷺ continues to show his love for his followers, which is why he is still alive in their hearts. It should be no surprise that no Muslim can bear insults to his esteemed person – no matter how minor it may be – as their love for him is deeply rooted in their hearts and is much greater than their love for their own mother and father.

The Muslims' love and devotion for the beloved Prophet ﷺ is nothing but a reflection of the Prophet's own love and mercy toward them. For example, on one occasion, whilst reciting the Qur'ān, he ﷺ recited the words of Jesus: ﴾*(O God!) If you punish them, then they are Your slaves, and if You forgive them, then verily You are Might and Wise.*﴿ [Q.5:118.] The Prophet ﷺ then raised his blessed hands and wept for his followers saying, "O God! My nation! My nation!" God sent the Archangel Gabriel to ask the Prophet ﷺ what was the matter and he ﷺ asked for the salvation of his followers. And so, God told Gabriel: "Go to Muhammad and say: 'Verily, We will please you with regard to your nation and We will not displease you.'"[1]

[1] Set forth by •Muslim in *al-Ṣaḥīḥ*, 1:191 §202. •al-Nasā'ī in *al-Sunan al-Kubrā*, 6:373 §11269. •Abū ʿAwāna in *al-Musnad*, 1:138 §415.

49

The One Who Greeted Others Warmly

One of the most beloved practices to the beloved Prophet Muhammad ﷺ was the greetings of peace. Whenever the Prophet ﷺ would meet others he would be the first to greet them with the greetings of peace[1] and he ﷺ would meet them by shaking their hands.[2] He ﷺ enjoined on his followers to greet each other in the same way and to spread the greetings of peace to those they know and those they do not know.[3]

It was reported that the Prophet ﷺ would smile when he would meet others. Whenever he ﷺ knocked on someone's door, he would never stand in front of the door, but he would keep a little distance and stand on its sides so as to not frighten the person opening and to give them space.[4] If someone called out to him, he would not turn his face only, but he would turn his whole body towards that person and give them his whole attention.[5]

---

[1] Set forth by •al-Tirmidhī in *al-Shamā'il al-Muḥammadiyya*, p. 38 §8. •al-Ṭabarānī in *al-Mu'jam al-Kabīr*, 22:156 §414.

[2] Set forth by •Abū Dāwūd in *al-Sunan*, 4:354 §5214.

[3] Set forth by •al-Bukhārī in *al-Ṣaḥīḥ*, 5:2302 §5882.

[4] Set forth by •Abū Dāwūd in *al-Sunan*, 4:348 §5186.

[5] Set forth by •al-Tirmidhī in *al-Shamā'il al-Muḥammadiyya*, p. 38 §8. •al-Ṭabarānī in *al-Mu'jam al-Kabīr*, 22:156 §414.

50

The Lover of Knowledge and Wisdom

"Wisdom is the lost property of the believer, let him claim it wherever he finds it," the Prophet Muhammad ﷺ said.[1] He ﷺ obligated the seeking of knowledge for all Muslims, saying: "Seeking knowledge is a duty upon every Muslim,"[2] and he ﷺ warned against hiding knowledge and withholding it, saying: "He who is asked about something he knows and conceals it will have a bridle of fire put on him on the day of resurrection."[3]

The esteemed Prophet Muhammad ﷺ encouraged Muslims to seek knowledge. He ﷺ said: "He who seeks knowledge and attains it will have a double portion of reward, but if he does not attain it, he will have a single portion of reward,"[4] and "If anyone seeks knowledge, it will be an atonement for past sins."[5]

---

[1] Set forth by •al-Tirmidhī in *al-Sunan*, 5:51 §2687. •Ibn Mājah in *al-Sunan*, 2:1395 §4169.

[2] Set forth by •Ibn Mājah in *al-Sunan*, 1:81 §224. •Abū Yaʿlā in *al-Musnad*, 7:96 §4035.

[3] Set forth by •Aḥmad b. Ḥanbal in *al-Musnad*, 2:263 §7561. •Abū Dāwūd in *al-Sunan*, 3:321 §3658. •Ibn Mājah in *al-Sunan*, 1:97 §264.

[4] Set forth by •al-Dārimī in *al-Sunan*, 1:108 §335.

[5] Set forth by •al-Tirmidhī in *al-Sunan*, 5:29 §2648. •al-Dārimī in *al-Sunan*, 1:149 §561.

51

The Advocate for the Environment

The Prophet ﷺ said, "If a Muslim plants a tree or sows seeds, and then a bird, or a person or an animal eats from it, it is regarded as a charitable gift for him."[1] He ﷺ also said: "If the Hour (the Day of Resurrection) is about to be established and one of you was holding a palm shoot, let him take advantage of even one second before the Hour is established[2] to plant it."[3] He ﷺ also prohibited cutting the trees of Mecca and Medina[4] and declared them as sanctuaries and forbade uprooting trees during warfare.[5]

---

[1] Set forth by •al-Bukhārī in *al-Ṣaḥīḥ*, 2:817 §2195. •Muslim in *al-Ṣaḥīḥ*, 3:1189 §1553.

[2] Set forth by •ʿAbd b. Ḥumayd in *al-Musnad*, p. 366 §1216. •al-Hindī in *Kanz al-ʿUmmāl*, 3:360 §9056.

[3] Set forth by •al-Bukhārī in *al-Ṣaḥīḥ*, 2:651 §1735. •Muslim in *al-Ṣaḥīḥ*, 2:987 §1354.

[4] Set forth by •al-Bukhārī in *al-Ṣaḥīḥ*, 2:661 §1768. •Muslim in *al-Ṣaḥīḥ*, 2:994 §1366. •Aḥmad b. Ḥanbal in *al-Musnad*, 3:393 §15270.

[5] Set forth by •Abū Dāwūd in *al-Sunan*, 3:41 §2629.

52

The Teacher of Hygiene

Prophet Muhammad ﷺ would teach his followers to observe high standards of hygiene. He ﷺ encouraged them to wash before every prayer and to clean their mouth.[1] He ﷺ avoided food that caused strong odours such as onions,[2] and commanded people to have a bath and wear clean clothes when coming to the mosque for the Friday prayer.[3] He ﷺ also taught his followers to observe cleanliness after visiting the toilet and to take care from getting one's body or clothes sullied.[4] From his practices, he ﷺ would wash his hands before eating and wash them afterwards.[5]

---

[1] Set forth by •al-Bukhārī in *al-Ṣaḥīḥ*, 1:303 §847. •Muslim in *al-Ṣaḥīḥ*, 1:220 §252.

[2] Set forth by •al-Bukhārī in *al-Ṣaḥīḥ*, 5:2077 §5137. •Muslim in *al-Ṣaḥīḥ*, 3:1623 §2053.

[3] Set forth by •al-Bukhārī in *al-Ṣaḥīḥ*, 1:301 §843. •Aḥmad b. Ḥanbal in *al-Musnad*, 5:438 §23761.

[4] Set forth by •al-Dāraquṭnī in *al-Sunan*, 1:127 §1, 2.

[5] Set forth by •Aḥmad b. Ḥanbal in *al-Musnad*, 5:441 §23783. •Abū Dāwūd in *al-Sunan*, 3:345 §3761.

53

The Founder of the First Constitution

When Prophet Muhammad ﷺ migrated to Medina, he formed a political alliance with the Jews, Christians and other non-Muslim minorities residing in Medina. He ﷺ drafted a formal agreement aimed at bringing an end to the bitter cycles of violence between the conflicting clans. This document, famously known as the 'Constitution of Medina, became the first written constitution in human history.[1]

[1] Set forth by •Abū ʿUbayd al-Qāsim b. Sallām in *Kitāb al-Amwāl*, pp. 166, 260 §328, 518. •Ḥumayd b. Zanjawayh in *Kitāb al-Amwāl*, 1:331 §508; 2:466 §750. •al-Bayhaqī in *al-Sunan al-Kubrā*, 8:106 §16147. •Ibn Hishām in *al-Sīra al-Nabawiyya*, 3:31. •Ibn Sayyid al-Nās in *ʿUyūn al-Athar*, 1:227. •Ibn Taymiyya in *al-Ṣārim al-Maslūl ʿalā Shātim al-Rasūl*, 2:129. •al-Ṣāliḥī in *Subul al-Hudā wa al-Rishād*, 3:555.

54

The Great Manager

Prophet Muhammad ﷺ gave the following commands to bring ease in times of difficulty: On a rainy day, he ﷺ advised the people to offer Friday prayers at home;[1] during a plague, he ﷺ asked people to quarantine and to maintain social distancing by not visiting or leaving the area.[2] He ﷺ opened the state treasury to provide people basic needs and appealed to the people to donate generously. He ﷺ started a soup kitchen to feed those who were unable to care for themselves. He ﷺ appointed a team of volunteers to facilitate timely disbursement of life necessities. He ﷺ admonished traders and merchants not to hoard or price gouge during times of crisis. He ﷺ urged people to consult medical experts. He ﷺ also advised following hygienic rules, not limited to the washing of hands five times a day during *wuḍū'*. He ﷺ also advised against throwing garbage in public places, ordering that it be disposed of safely.

---

[1] Set forth by •al-Bukhārī in *al-Ṣaḥīḥ*, 1:306 §859. •Muslim in *al-Ṣaḥīḥ*, 1:485 §699.

[2] Set forth by •al-Bukhārī in *al-Ṣaḥīḥ*, 5:2163 §5396. •Aḥmad b. Ḥanbal in *al-Musnad*, 1:180 §1554.

55

The Advocate of Moderation

"Beware of going to extremes in the religion, for the only thing that destroyed those before you was extremism in religion,"[1] the Prophet warned. The Companions relate that he ordered them to adhere to a moderate path and not to make religion difficult, otherwise it would overcome them.[2] He taught moderation in religion, by advising his followers to practice the religion as much as they can bear and not to go into extremes.[3]

He also taught that excesses, be they in acts of worship or in personal dealings, are to be avoided. It is reported that he once said, "Stick to the actions you can bear, for God does not tire till you tire. Indeed, the most beloved actions in the sight of God are those that are the most consistent, even if they are little."[4]

---

1 Set forth by •Aḥmad b. Ḥanbal in *al-Musnad*, 1:215 §1851. •al-Nasāʾī in *al-Sunan*, 5:268 §3057.

2 Set forth by •al-Bukhārī in *al-Ṣaḥīḥ*, 1:23 §39. •al-Nasāʾī in *al-Sunan*, 8:122 §5034.

3 Set forth by •al-Bukhārī in *al-Ṣaḥīḥ*, 5:2373 §6098. •Ibn al-Jaʿd in *al-Musnad*, 1:407 §2773.

4 Set forth by •al-Bukhārī in *al-Ṣaḥīḥ*, 5:2201 §5523. •Muslim in *al-Ṣaḥīḥ*, 1:540 §782.

56

The Teacher of Self-Restraint

"The great striver in the way of God is he who strives against his lower self," the Prophet Muhammad ﷺ said. According to the Prophet ﷺ striving against one's ego and learning self-restraint are the greatest things that one can strive for.[1] In another narration, the Prophet Muhammad ﷺ addressed toxic behaviour and reset the balance of true masculinity by encouraging men to show self-restraint and to learn to control their anger. He ﷺ said: "The strong man is not one who is good at wrestling, but the strong man is one who controls himself in a fit of rage."[2]

---

[1] Set forth by •Aḥmad b. Ḥanbal in *al-Musnad*, 2:128 §6116. •Ibn Mājah in *al-Sunan*, 2:1401 §4189.

[2] Set forth by •al-Bukhārī in *al-Ṣaḥīḥ*, 5:2267 §5763. •Muslim in *al-Ṣaḥīḥ*, 4:2014 §2609.

57

The Encourager of Cooperation in Goodness

The Prophet ﷺ adopted the following Qurʾānic principle: ﴾*And always support one another in (the works of) righteousness and piety, but do not become accomplices in (works of) sin and transgression.*﴿ [Q.5:2.] He ﷺ said: "If anyone relieves a Muslim believer from one of the hardships of this worldly life, God will relieve him of one of the hardships of the Day of Resurrection. If anyone makes it easy for the one who is indebted to him (while finding it difficult to repay), God will make it easy for him in this worldly life and in the Hereafter, and if anyone conceals the faults of a Muslim, God will conceal his faults in this world and in the Hereafter. God helps His slave as long as he helps his brother."[1]

[1] Set forth by •Muslim in *al-Ṣaḥīḥ*, 4:2074 §2699. •Aḥmad b. Ḥanbal in *al-Musnad*, 2:252 §7421. •Abū Dāwūd in *al-Sunan*, 4:287 §4946.

58

The Introducer of Justness in Warfare

The Prophet ﷺ never resorted to fighting in self-defence unless it was the last resort. He ﷺ set limitations to warfare by placing many rules around it. For example, he forbade the killing of non-combatants saying: "Go in God's name, trusting in God, and adhering to the religion of God's Apostle. Do not kill a decrepit old man, or a young infant, or a child, or a woman; do not be dishonest about booty, but collect your spoils, do right and act well, for God loves those who do well."[1]

This limitation in self-defence also extended to other religious communities as the Prophet ﷺ forbade the killing of monks and priests and destroying places of worship.[2] He ﷺ also forbade the destruction of the environment by forbidding the uprooting of forests and trees or burning crops or fields.[3] Likewise, he ﷺ also prohibited the killing of merchants and traders[4] as it would affect the supply of food to the common people and cause undue difficulty and hardship.

[1] Set forth by •al-Bayhaqī in *al-Sunan al-Kubrā*, 9:90 §17934. •al-Hindī in *Kanz al-ʿUmmāl*, 4:205 §11425.

[2] Set forth by •Ibn Abī Shayba in *al-Muṣannaf*, 6:484 §33132. •Abū Yaʿlā in *al-Musnad*, 5:59 §2650.

[3] Set forth by •al-Bayhaqī in *al-Sunan al-Kubrā*, 9:90 §17934. •al-Hindī in *Kanz al-ʿUmmāl*, 4:205 §11425.

[4] Set forth by •Ibn Abī Shayba in *al-Muṣannaf*, 6:484 §33130. •al-Bayhaqī in *al-Sunan al-Kubrā*, 9:91 §17939.

59

The Rejecter of Hoarding and Wasting

"Do not hoard; otherwise, God will withhold from you," the Prophet ﷺ warned his followers. Hoarding resources and provisions is harmful to society, and this is contrary to the teachings of Islam. The Prophet Muhammad ﷺ strictly condemned such practices.[1] He ﷺ taught his followers not to hike prices saying, "and do not go ahead to meet the caravan (for buying the goods, but wait) till it reaches the market."[2] This command was to stop prices from being raised and a monopoly being developed, because society should be built on a fair and just distribution between all members of society.

Likewise, the Prophet ﷺ disliked waste, even if there was no fear of that resource being depleted. For example, the esteemed Prophet ﷺ said: "Do not waste water even if you were at a running stream."[3] Even if a resource was unlimited, he ﷺ taught us to preserve it and to be mindful of how we make use of it, lest one day God takes this blessing away from us. Thus, avoiding waste is a way to be thankful of God's blessings, and this is what the Prophet ﷺ taught his followers.

---

[1] Set forth by •Muslim in *al-Ṣaḥīḥ*, 3:1227 §1605. •Aḥmad b. Ḥanbal in *al-Musnad*, 3:453 §15796.

[2] Set forth by •al-Bukhārī in *al-Ṣaḥīḥ*, 2:758 §2054.

[3] Set forth by •Aḥmad b. Ḥanbal in *al-Musnad*, 2:221 §7065. •Ibn Mājah in *al-Sunan*, 1:147 §425.

60

The Best in Handling Criticism

The Jewish Rabbi, Zayd b. Saʿna, wanted to test the patience of the Prophet ﷺ to see if he truly was the Prophet of God. He lent the Prophet ﷺ money, which was promised to be paid back on a certain date. However, Zayd b. Saʿna came to the Prophet ﷺ before the set date and asked for his money back, but his treatment towards the Prophet ﷺ was very harsh and he used some offensive words. Hearing this, the Companion ʿUmar ؓ got angry and stood up to confront the Rabbi, however the esteemed Prophet ﷺ said: "[O ʿUmar!] This man is entitled to better treatment from you. You ought to have advised me to repay the loan promptly and asked him to make his demand politely."[1]

[1] Set forth by •Abū al-Shaykh al-Aṣbahānī in *Akhlāq al-Nabī* ﷺ *wa Ādābihi*, 1:475 §178.

61

The Best User of His Time

The Prophet ﷺ taught the importance of time. From his own example, he divided his time proportionally for the worship of God, service to his family and his own self – and even then, he ﷺ would share his personal time with others. He ﷺ would sacrifice his own leisure time to help others and to provide them comfort. Most of his days were spent teaching and educating his Companions ﷺ, such that they would come to him in a state of ignorance and return from his gatherings as scholars and jurists.[1]

[1] Set forth by •al-Ṭabarānī in *al-Aḥādīth al-Ṭawāl*, 1:245 §29; & in *al-Muʿjam al-Kabīr*, 22:157 §414. •al-Haythamī in *Majmaʿ al-Zawāʾid*, 8:274. •al-Hindī in *Kanz al-ʿUmmāl*, 7:64 §18535.

62

His Teachings

The Prophet Muhammad ﷺ commanded the good and forbade the evil. The following are some of his teachings:

One of the Prophet's Companions ﷺ said: "God's Prophet ﷺ took (a pledge) from us as he took from the women that we will not associate any partners with God and we will not steal, and we will not commit adultery, and we will not kill our children, and we will not bring calumny upon one another."[1]

According to another Companion, the Prophet ﷺ said: "If you observe your five times of prayer, fast during your month of Ramaḍān, pay the Zakat on your properties and obey him who has a right to issue commands to you, you will enter your Lord's Paradise."[2]

He ﷺ also said: "Feed the hungry, visit the ailing and release the one in captivity (by paying his ransom)."[3]

And: "By Him in Whose Hand my soul is! You will not enter Paradise until you believe, and you shall not believe until you love one another. May I inform you of something, if you do, you love each other? Promote the greeting of peace amongst you".[4]

---

[1] Set forth by •al-Bukhārī in *al-Ṣaḥīḥ*, 1:15 §18.

[2] Set forth by •Aḥmad b. Ḥanbal in *al-Musnad*, 5:251 §22215. •al-Tirmidhī in *al-Sunan*, 2:516 §616.

[3] Set forth by •al-Bukhārī in *al-Ṣaḥīḥ*, 5:2139 §5325. •Aḥmad b. Ḥanbal in *al-Musnad*, 4:394 §19535.

[4] Set forth by •Muslim in *al-Ṣaḥīḥ*, 1:74 §54.

From his teachings, is his statement: "A Muslim is a brother to a Muslim. He should neither deceive him nor lie to him, nor leave him without assistance. Everything belonging to a Muslim is inviolable for a Muslim; his honour, his blood and property. Piety is here (and he pointed to his chest thrice). It is enough for a Muslim to commit evil by despising his Muslim brother."[1]

[1] Set forth by •Aḥmad b. Ḥanbal in *al-Musnad*, 2:360 §8707.

63

His Golden Principles

Prophet Muhammad ﷺ was known for the comprehensiveness of his speech.[1] These comprehensive words were the golden principles of his teachings and they are bedrock of Islam. Among his comprehensive words are the following:

"Religion is sincerity,"[2]

"Do not cause harm or reciprocate harm."[3]

"Actions are by their intentions."[4]

"God is beautiful, and He loves beauty".[5]

"Whoever believes in God and the Last Day, let him say what is good, or remain silent."[6]

"Fear God wherever you may be. Follow a bad action with a good one to erase it. And treat people well."[7]

"Every human being makes a mistake. And the best of those who make mistakes are the ones who repent and ask

---

[1] Set forth by •Aḥmad b. Ḥanbal in *al-Musnad*, 2:172 §6606.

[2] Set forth by •al-Bayhaqī in *Shuʿab al-Īmān*, 6:25 §7400.

[3] Set forth by •Aḥmad b. Ḥanbal in *al-Musnad*, 1:313 §2867. •Ibn Mājah in *al-Sunan*, 2:784 §2341.

[4] Set forth by •al-Bukhārī in *al-Ṣaḥīḥ*, 1:3 §1.

[5] Set forth by •Muslim in *al-Ṣaḥīḥ*, 1:93 §91. •Aḥmad b. Ḥanbal in *al-Musnad*, 1:399 §3789.

[6] Set forth by •al-Bukhārī in *al-Ṣaḥīḥ*, 5:2376 §6110. •Muslim in *al-Ṣaḥīḥ*, 1:68 §47.

[7] Set forth by •Aḥmad b. Ḥanbal in *al-Musnad*, 5:153 §21392. •al-Tirmidhī in *al-Sunan*, 4:355 §1987.

forgiveness."[1]

"A good word is charity."[2]

"Be in this world like a stranger."[3]

"The one who encourages a good is like the one who acts upon it."[4]

---

[1] Set forth by •Aḥmad b. Ḥanbal in *al-Musnad*, 3:198 §13072. •al-Tirmidhī in *al-Sunan*, 4:659 §2499.

[2] Set forth by •al-Bukhārī in *al-Ṣaḥīḥ*, 3:1059 §2734. •Muslim in *al-Ṣaḥīḥ*, 2:699 §1009.

[3] Set forth by •al-Bukhārī in *al-Ṣaḥīḥ*, 5:2358 §6053. •Aḥmad b. Ḥanbal in *al-Musnad*, 2:24 §4764.

[4] Set forth by •Abū Nuʿaym in *Musnad Abī Ḥanīfa*, p. 151. •Abū Yaʿlā in *al-Musnad*, 7:275 §4296.

Bibliography

The Holy Qur'ān

Ibn ʿAbd al-Barr, Abū ʿUmar Yūsuf b. ʿAbd Allāh b. Muhammad (368–463/979–1071), *al-Istīʿāb fī Maʿrifa al-Aṣḥāb,* Beirut, Lebanon: Dār al-Jīl, 1412 AH.

ʿAbd al-Razzāq, Abū Bakr b. Hammām b. Nāfiʿ al-Ṣanʿānī (126–211/744–826), *al-Muṣannaf*, Beirut, Lebanon: al-Maktab al-Islāmī, 1403 AH.

ʿAbd b. Ḥumayd, Abū Muhammad b. Naṣr al-Kasī (d. 249/863), *al-Musnad*, Cairo, Egypt: Maktaba al-Sunna, 1408/1988.

Ibn Abī ʿĀṣim, Abū Bakr b. ʿAmr al-Ḍaḥḥāk b. Makhlad al-Shaybānī (206–287/822–900), *al-Sunna,* Beirut, Lebanon: al-Maktab al-Islāmī 1400 AH.

Ibn Abī al-Dunyā, *al-Ṣamt wa Ādāb al-Lisān.*

Ibn Abī Shayba, Abū Bakr ʿAbd Allāh b. Muhammad b. Ibrahīm b. ʿUthmān al-Kūfī (159–235/776–850), *al-Muṣannaf,* Riyadh, Saudi Arabia: Maktaba al-Rushd, 1409 AH.

Aḥmad b. Ḥanbal, Abū ʿAbd Allāh b. Muhammad (164–241/780–855), *al-Musnad*, Beirut, Lebanon: al-Maktab al-Islāmī, 1398/1978.

Abū ʿAwāna, Yaʿqūb b. Isḥāq b. Ibrāhīm b. Zayd al-Naysabūrī (230–316/845–928), *al-Musnad,* Beirut, Lebanon: Dār al-Maʿrifa, 1998.

Ibn ʿAsākir, Abū al-Qāsim ʿAlī b. al-Ḥasan b. Hibat Allāh b. ʿAbd Allāh b. al-Ḥusayn al-Dimashqī (499–571/1105–1176), *Tārīkh Dimashq al-Kabīr,* generally known as *Tārīkh Ibn ʿAsākīr,* Beirut, Lebanon: Dār al-Iḥyā' al-Turāth al-ʿArabī, 1421/2001.

al-Baghawī, Abū Muhammad al-Ḥusayn b. Masʿūd b. Muhammad (436–516/1044–1122), *Maʿālim al-Tanzīl,* Beirut, Lebanon: Dār

al-Maʿrifa, 1407/1987.
al-Bayhaqī, Abū Bakr Aḥmad b. al-Ḥusayn b. ʿAlī b. ʿAbd Allāh b. Mūsā (384–458/994–1066), *Dalāʾil al-Nubuwwa*, Beirut, Lebanon: Dār al-Kutub al-ʿIlmiyya, 1405/1985.
—. *Shuʿab al-Īmān*, Beirut, Lebanon: Dār al-Kutub al-ʿIlmiyya, 1410/1990.
—. *al-Sunan al-Kubrā*, Mecca, Saudi Arabia: Maktaba Dār al-Bāz, 1414/1994.
al-Bayjūrī, *al-Muwāhib al-Laduniyya ʿalā al-Shamāʾil al-Muhammadiyya*.
al-Bazzār, Abū Bakr Aḥmad b. ʿAmr b. ʿAbd al-Khāliq al-Baṣrī (210–292/825–905), *al-Musnad*, Beirut, Lebanon: 1409 AH.
al-Bukhārī, Abū ʿAbd Allāh Muhammad b. Ismāʿīl b. Ibrahīm b. Mughīra (194–256/810–870), *al-Adab al-Mufrad*, Beirut, Lebanon: Dār al-Bashāʾir al-Islāmiyya, 1409/1989.
—. *al-Ṣaḥīḥ*, Beirut, Lebanon, Damascus, Syria: Dār al-Qalam, 1401/1981.
al-Dāraquṭnī, Abū al-Ḥasan ʿAlī b. ʿUmar b. Aḥmad b. al-Mahdī b. Masʿūd b. al-Nuʿmān (306–385/918–995), *al-Sunan,* Beirut, Lebanon: Dār al-Maʿrifa, 1386/1966.
al-Dārimī, Abū Muhammad ʿAbd Allāh b. ʿAbd al-Raḥmān (181–255/797–869), *al-Sunan*, Beirut, Lebanon: Dār al-Kitāb al-ʿArabī, 1407 AH.
Abū Dāwūd, Sulaymān b. Ashʿath b. Isḥāq b. Bashīr al-Sijistānī (202–275/817–889), *al-Sunan*, Beirut, Lebanon: Dār al-Fikr, 1414/1994.
—.*al-Marāsīl*, Beirut, Lebanon: Muʾassasa al-Risāla, 1408 AH.
al-Ghazālī, Abū Ḥāmid Muhammad b. Muhammad al-Ghazālī (450–505 AH), *Iḥyāʾ ʿUlūm al-Dīn,* Beirut, Lebanon: Dār al-Maʿrifa.
al-Ḥākim, Abū ʿAbd Allāh Muhammad b. ʿAbd Allāh b. Muhammad (321–405/933–1014), *al-Mustadrak ʿalā al-Ṣaḥīḥayn*, Beirut, Lebanon: Dār al-Kutub al-ʿIlmiyya, 1411/1990.
al-Ḥalabī, ʿAlī b. Burhān al-Dīn (d. 1404 AH), *Insān al-ʿUyūn fī*

Sīra al-Amīn al-Maʾmūn (al-Sīra al-Ḥalabiyya), Beirut, Lebanon: Dār al-Maʿrifa, 1400 AH.
al-Ḥārith, Ibn Abī Usāma (186–282/802–895), *Baghyat al-Bāḥith ʿan Zawāʾid Musnad al-Ḥārith*, Medina, Saudi Arabia: Markz Khidma al-Sunna wa al-Sīra al-Nabawiyya, 1413/1992.
al-Haythamī, Nūr al-Dīn Abū al-Ḥasan ʿAlī b. Abī Bakr b. Sulaymān (735–807/1335–1405), *Majmaʿ al-Zawāʾid*, Cairo, Egypt: Dār al-Riyān li al-Turāth & Beirut Lebanon: Dār al-Kitab al-ʿArabī, 1407/1987.
Ibn Ḥibbān, Abū Ḥātim Muhammad b. Ḥibbān b. Aḥmad b. Ḥibbān (270–354/884–965), *al-Ṣaḥīḥ*, Beirut, Lebanon: Muʾassisa al-Risāla, 1414/1993.
—. *al-Thiqāt*, Beirut, Lebanon: Dār al-Fikr, 1395 AH.
al-Hindī, ʿAlāʾ al-Dīn ʿAlī b. Ḥussām al-Dīn al-Muttaqī (d. 975 AH), *Kanz al-ʿUmmāl fī Sunan al-Afāl wa al-Aqwāl,* Beirut, Lebanon: Muʾassisa al-Risāla, 1399/1979.
Ibn Hishām, Abū Muhammad ʿAbd al-Malik (d. 213/828), *al-Sīra al-Nabawiyya,* Beirut, Lebanon: Dār al-Jīl,1411 AH.
al-Ḥumaydī, Abū Bakr Muhammad b. Isḥāq (219/834), *al-Musnad*, Beirut, Lebanon: Dār al-Kutub al-ʿIlmiyya.
Ibn al-Jaʿd, Abū al-Ḥasan ʿAlī b. Jaʿd b. ʿUbayd Hāshimī (133–230/750–845), *al-Musnad,* Beirut, Lebanon: Muʾassisa Nādir, 1410/1990.
Ibn Kathīr, Abū al-Fidāʾ Ismāʿīl b. ʿUmar (701–774/1301–1373), *Tafsīr al-Qurʾān al-ʿAẓīm,* Beirut, Lebanon: Dār al-Maʿrifa, 1400/1980.
al-Khaṭīb al-Baghdādı, Abū Bakr Aḥmad b. ʿAlī b. Thābit b. Aḥmad b. al-Mahdī b. Thābit (392–463/1002–1071), *Tārīkh Baghdād*, Beirut, Lebanon: Dār al Kutāb al-ʿIlmiyya.
Ibn Khuzayma, Abū Bakr Muhammad b. Isḥāq (223–311/838–924), *al-Ṣaḥīḥ*, Beirut, Lebanon: al-Maktab al-Islāmī, 1390/1970.
Ibn Mājah, Abū ʿAbd Allāh Muhammad b. Yazīd al-Qazwīnī (209–273/824–887), *al-Sunan*, Beirut, Lebanon: Dār al-Kutub al-ʿIlmiyya, 1419/1998.

al-Maqdisī, Muhammad b. ʿAbd al-Wāḥid al-Ḥanbalī, (567–643 AH), *al-Aḥādīth al-Mukhtāra,* Mecca, Saudi Arabia: Maktaba al-Nahda al-Ḥadīthiyya, 1410/1990.
al-Mundhirī, Abū Muhammad ʿAbd al-Aẓīm b. ʿAbd al-Qawī b. ʿAbd Allāh b. Salama b. Saʿd (581–656/1185–1258), *al-Targhīb wa al-Tarhīb,* Beirut, Lebanon: Dār al-Kutub al-ʿIlmiyya, 1417 AH.
Muslim, Ibn al-Ḥajjāj Abū al-Ḥusayn al-Qushayrī al-Naysābūrī (206–261/821–875), *al-Ṣaḥīḥ*, Beirut, Lebanon: Dār al-Iḥyāʾ al-Turāth al-ʿArabī.
al-Nasāʾī, Aḥmad b. Shuʿayb Abū ʿAbd al-Raḥmān (215–303/830–915), *al-Sunan,* Beirut, Lebanon: Dār al-Kutub al-ʿIlmiyya, 1416/1995.
—. *al-Sunan al-Kubrā*, Beirut, Lebanon: Dār al-Kutub al-ʿIlmiyya, 1411/1991.
Abū Nuʿaym, Aḥmad b. ʿAbd Allāh b. Aḥmad b. Isḥāq b. Mūsā b. Mihrān al-Aṣbahānī (336–430/948–1038), *Dalāʾil al-Nubuwwa*, Hyderabad, India: Majlis Dāʾira Maʿārif ʿUthmāniyya.
—. *Musnad al-Imām Abī Ḥanīfa*, Riyad, Saudi Arabia, Maktaba al-Kawthar, 1415 AH.
—.*Maʿrifat al-Ṣaḥāba*, Riyadh, Saudi Arabia: Dār al-Waṭan liʾl-Nashr, 1419 AH/1998 CE.
al-Qāḍī ʿIyāḍ, Abū al-Faḍl ʿIyāḍ b. Mūsā b. ʿIyāḍ b. ʿAmr b. Mūsā b. ʿIyāḍ b. Muhammad b. Mūsā b. ʿIyāḍ al-Yaḥṣubī (476–544/1083–1149), *al-Shifāʾ bi-Taʿrīf Ḥuqūq al-Muṣṭafā* ﷺ, Beirut, Lebanon: Dār al-Kitab al-ʿArabī.
al-Qasṭallānī, Abū al-ʿAbbās Aḥmad b. Muhammad b. Abī Bakr b. ʿAbd al-Malik b. Aḥmad b. Muhammad b. Muhammad b. Ḥusayn b. ʿAlī (851–923/1448–1517), *al-Mawāhib al-Laduniyya bi al-Minḥ al-Muhammadiyya*, Beirut, Lebanon: al-Maktab al-Islamī, 1412/1991.
al-Qurṭubī, Abū ʿAbd Allāh Muhammad b. Aḥmad b. Muhammad b. Yaḥyā b. Mufarraj al-Umawī (d. 671 AH), *al-Jāmiʿ li-Aḥkām al-Qurʾān,* Beirut, Lebanon: Dār al-Iḥyāʾ al-Turāth al-ʿArabī.
al-Rāghib al-Aṣfahānī, Abū al-Qāsim al-Ḥusyan b. Muhammad

(d. 502 AH), *al-Mufradāt*, Beirut, Lebanon: Dār al-Qalam, 1412 AH.

Ibn Rāhawayh, Abū Yaʿqūb Isḥāq b. Ibrahīm b. Makhlad b. Ibrahīm b. ʿAbd Allāh (161–237/778–851), *al-Musnad*, Medina, Saudi Arabia: Maktaba al-Īmān, 1412/1991.

Ibn Rāshid, Maʿmar b. Rāshid al-Azdī (d. 151 AH), *al-Jāmiʿ*, Beirut, Lebanon: al-Maktab al-Islāmī, 1403 AH.

al-Rūyānī, Abū Bakr Muhammad b. Hārūn (d. 307 AH), *al-Musnad*, Cairo, Egypt: Muʾassisa Cordoba, 1416 AH.

Ibn Saʿd, Abū ʿAbd Allāh Muhammad (168–230/784–845), *al-Ṭabaqāt al-Kubrā,* Beirut, Lebanon: Dār Beirut li al-Ṭabat wa al-Nashr, 1398/1978.

al-Ṣāliḥī, Muhammad b. Yūsuf al-Ṣāliḥī al-Dimashqī al-Shāfiʿī (d. 942 AH), *Subul al-Hudā wa al-Rishād*, Beirut, Lebanon: Dār al-Kutub al-ʿIlmiyya, 1414 AH/1993CE.

al-Shāfiʿī, Abū ʿAbd Allāh Muhammad b. Idrīs b. ʿAbbās b. ʿUthmān b. al-Shāfiʿ al-Qurashī (150–204/767–819), *al-Musnad,* Beirut, Lebanon: Dār al-Kutub al-ʿIlmiyya.

al-Shawkānī, Muhammad b. ʿAlī b. Muhammad (1173–1250/1760–1834), *Nayl al-Awṭār Sharḥ Muntaqā al-Akhbār,* Beirut, Lebanon: Dār al-Fikr, 1402/1982.

Abū al-Shaykh al-Aṣbahānī, Abū Muhammad ʿAbd Allāh b. Muhammad b. Jaʿfar b. Ḥayyān al-Anṣārī (d. 369 AH), *Akhlāq al-Nabī ﷺ wa Ādābihi*, Dār al-Muslim liʾl-Nashr wa al-Tawzīʿ, 1998 CE.

Ibn al-Sunnī, Aḥmad b. Muhammad al-Daynūrī (284–364 AH), *ʿAmal al-Yawm wa al-Layla,* Beirut, Lebanon: Dār Ibn Ḥazm, 1425/2004.

al-Suyūṭī, Jalāl al-Dīn Abū al-Faḍl ʿAbd al-Raḥmān b. Abī Bakr b. Muhammad b. Abī Bakr b. ʿUthmān (849–911/1445–1505), *al-Khaṣāʾiṣ al-Kubrā,* Faisalabad, Pakistan: Maktaba al-Nūriyya al-Riḍwiyya.

—. *al-Riyāḍ al-Anīqa fī Sharḥ Asmāʾ Khayr al-Khalīqa.*

—. *al-Shamāʾil al-Sharīfa*, Dār Ṭāʾir al-ʿIlm liʾl-Nashr wa al-Tawzīʿ.

al-Ṭabarānī, Abū al-Qāsim Sulaymān b. Aḥmad b. Ayyūb b. Maṭīr al-Lakhmī (260–360/873–971), *Kitāb al-Duʿāʾ*, Beirut, Lebanon: Dār al-Kutub al-ʿIlmiyya, 1421/2001.
—. *al-Muʿjam al-Awsaṭ*, Riyadh, Saudi Arabia: Maktaba al-Maʿārif, 1405/1985.
—. *al-Muʿjam al-Kabīr*, Mosul, Iraq: Matbaʿa al-Zahrāʾ al-Ḥadītha.
—. *Musnad al-Shāmiyyīn*, Beirut, Lebanon: Muʾassisa al-Risāla, 1405/1985.
—. *al-Aḥādīth al-Ṭawāl*, Mosul, Iraq, Maktaba al-Zahrāʾ, 1404 AH/1983 CE.
al-Ṭabarī, Abū Jaʿfar Aḥmad Muhammad b. Jarīr b. Yazīd (224–310/839–923), *Tārīkh al-Umam wa al-Mulūk*, Beirut, Lebanon: Dār al-Kutub al-ʿIlmiyya, 1407 AH.
Tamām al-Rāzī, *al-Fawāʾid*.
al-Ṭayālisī, Abū Dāwūd Sulaymān b. Dāwūd al-Jārūd (133–204/751–819), *al-Musnad*, Beirut, Lebanon: Dār al-Maʿrifa.
al-Tirmidhī, Abū ʿĪsā Muhammad b. ʿĪsā b. Sūra b. Mūsā b. Ḍaḥḥāk Salmā (210–279/825–892), *al-Shamāʾil al-Muhammadiyya wa Khaṣāʾiṣ al-Muṣṭfawiyya*, Beirut, Lebanon: Muʾassisa al-Kutub al-Thaqāfiyya, 1412 AH.
—. *al-Sunan*, Beirut, Lebanon: Dār al-Gharb al-Islāmī, 1998.
Abū Yaʿlā, Aḥmad b. ʿAlī b. Mathnā b. Yaḥyā b. ʿĪsā b. al-Hilāl al-Mūṣilī al-Tamīmī (210–307/825–919), *al-Musnad*, Damascus, Syria: Dār al-Maʾmūn li al-Turāth, 1404/1984.